A
CHURCH
ON THE
MOVE

Tim + Pat,
God's blessings!
Joe Paprocki

Other Books by Joe Paprocki

*The Catechist's Toolbox: How to Thrive as a
Religious Education Teacher*

*La caja de herramientas del catequista: cómo triunfar en el
ministerio de la catequesis*

*Beyond the Catechist's Toolbox: Catechesis That Not Only
Informs but Also Transforms*

*Más allá de la caja de herramientas del catequista:
catequesis que no solo informa, sino que también transforma*

*The Bible Blueprint: A Catholic's Guide to Understanding
and Embracing God's Word*

*Los planos de la Biblia: una guía católica para entender y
acoger la Palabra de Dios*

*Living the Mass: How One Hour a Week Can Change Your
Life (with Fr. Dominic Grassi)*

*Vivir la misa: cómo una hora a la semana puede combiar tu
vida (con el Padre Dominic Grassi)*

*Practice Makes Catholic: Moving from a Learned Faith
to a Lived Faith*

*Under the Influence of Jesus: The Transforming Experience
of Encountering Christ*

*7 Keys to Spiritual Wellness: Enriching Your Faith by
Strengthening the Health of Your Soul*

*A Well-Built Faith: A Catholic's Guide to Knowing and
Sharing What We Believe*

*Una fe bien construida: guía católica para conocer y
compartir lo que creemos*

A CHURCH ON THE MOVE

52 WAYS to Get Mission
and Mercy in Motion

JOE PAPROCKI, DMIN

LOYOLA PRESS.
A JESUIT MINISTRY
Chicago

LOYOLA PRESS.
A JESUIT MINISTRY

3441 N. Ashland Avenue
Chicago, Illinois 60657
(800) 621-1008
www.loyolapress.com

Scripture passages cited as *New International Version* translation are taken from *Holy Bible, New International Version*®. Copyright © 1973, 1978, 1984 by International Bible Society. Used by permission of Zondervan Publishing House. All rights reserved.

The "NIV" and "New International Version" trademarks are registered in the United States Patent and Trademark Office by the International Bible Society. Use of either trademark requires the permission of the International Bible Society.

Cover art credit: © iStock/chinaface
Interior illustration by John L. Paprocki.

ISBN-13: 978-0-8294-4405-6
ISBN-10: 0-8294-4405-X
Library of Congress Control Number: 2015959039

Printed in the United States of America.
16 17 18 19 20 21 22 Versa 10 9 8 7 6 5 4 3 2 1

To Fr. George Lane, SJ, President Emeritus of Loyola Press, the man who taught me the importance of saying the following three words every day: "Thank you, Jesus!"

Contents

I Believe This Is Going to Be
Our Finest Hour

Two lines from the movie *Apollo 13* come to mind as being quite apropos for describing what this book, *A Church on the Move*, is all about. The first is obvious: "Houston, we have a problem," the words uttered by astronaut James Lovell after an oxygen tank exploded, crippling the spacecraft on its journey to the moon and endangering the crew. As the damaged spacecraft pitched out of control and attempted to limp back to earth, mission control scrambled to figure out how to ensure that the three astronauts would indeed return home safely, which leads to the second, less well-known quote from the movie. Upon overhearing a fellow official at mission control lament that this could be the worst disaster NASA ever faced, Gene Kranz, NASA flight director at mission control, confidently replied, "With all due respect, sir, I believe this is gonna be our finest hour."

The Catholic Church has a problem. In a similar way that the Apollo 13 spacecraft was crippled by an explosion and leaking fuel, the Catholic Church has been crippled by the explosion of the priest sexual abuse crisis, growing secularism, and a new atheism, and, as a result, has been "leaking" members at an astonishing rate.

The extent of the problem has been diagnosed by study after study, revealing that, although most Christian churches are losing members, Catholicism is losing members at a higher rate than any other denomination (2014 Religious Landscape Study).

- For every one person who enters the Catholic Church, more than six Catholics leave.
- Four out of ten people who were brought up Catholic no longer identify with Catholicism.
- If former Catholics were considered a denomination, it would be the second-largest denomination in the U.S.

Like the NASA official who feared a disaster that would sound the end of space exploration, many believe that this is a disaster from which the church will not recover.

I'm not one of those people. Like Gene Kranz, the steadfast NASA flight director who believed that failure was not an option, I prefer to believe that we are about to enter our finest hour—a time in which the transforming grace of Jesus Christ will seize hold of the situation and lead us to new life. For that to happen, however, we need to enthusiastically and tirelessly hoist our sails to cooperate with the Holy Spirit's prevailing winds.

In order to bring home the astronauts of the crippled Apollo 13 spacecraft, Gene Kranz and mission control had to improvise. They revisited every item on board the spacecraft and determined how it could be repurposed to contribute to bringing the crew home safely. Directing them to use mundane objects such as a cardboard box, a couple of socks, a bag, parts from their space suits, a bungee cord, and duct tape, mission control enabled the astronauts to successfully rig a filtering device that prevented them from poisoning themselves with their own CO_2 on a lunar module that was designed to carry a crew of two for thirty-six hours as opposed to a crew of three for ninety-six hours. The Catholic Church needs to do something similar. We need to work the problem. We need to look at the resources we already have and determine how we can repurpose much of what is already in our possession. We need to pray for the grace to employ creativity and ingenuity. And most of all, we need to adapt to the real conditions surrounding us or risk poisoning ourselves with our own despair.

In recent years, several popular books and seminars have proposed ways to "rebuild" and "renovate" the church to get it moving again so that it can become more like the burgeoning evangelical Protestant megachurches to which so many ex-Catholics are going. Unfortunately, these approaches tend to be personality driven. While we can indeed learn a number of valuable lessons from these megachurches, too many of our priests are now suffocating under the unrealistic expectations that they need to become Rick Warren, Bill Hybels, Joel Osteen, T. D. Jakes, and Joyce Meyer all rolled into one. That is not a knock against our pastors. The reality is that most of them are good, decent, holy, simple men. They are not rock stars, nor should they be. The Catholic Church has long been suspicious, and rightly so, of the cult of personality, which is why our pastors and priests are transferred every so often. On the one hand, this practice has avoided, for the most part, the problems that come with the rock-star pastor—namely, the collapse of the congregation upon the pastor's retirement, resignation, or death. On the other hand, this practice has all too often fostered a culture of mediocrity in many of our Catholic parishes because pastors come and go and emphases and priorities get shifted according to their tastes and whims.

While we most certainly should have (and deserve) outstanding pastors, the fact is, most effective Catholic parishes do not succeed because the pastor is a rock star but because the parish as a whole is discovering creative and ingenious approaches to tapping into the power of God's extraordinary grace in ordinary ways. So the key to having a church on the move is not to wait for the messiah-pastor to arrive. Nor is it to remodel the sanctuary, open a café, hire ten professional musicians, or install giant projection screens for use at all liturgies—as good as some of these things may be. The key is to focus on the one treasure the parish can deliver that secular society cannot, and that one treasure is Jesus Christ.

The vision for how to achieve a church on the move has been laid out by Pope Francis through his actions and words, most notably, his Apostolic Letter *Evangelii Gaudium*—"The Joy of the Gospel." His message has resonated with people all over the world and created an excitement about the Catholic Church that many refer to as the "Francis effect." I find it very surprising, then, to discover that not a few bishops have felt confused about what Francis is asking the church to do and be. This confusion was best summed up by the late Francis Cardinal George, former archbishop of Chicago, who commented just a few months before his death that Pope Francis "says wonderful things, but he doesn't put them together all the time, so you're left at times puzzling over what his intention is. What he says is clear enough, but what does he want us to do?" ("U.S. Bishops Struggle to Follow Lead of Francis," *New York Times*, November 11, 2014). I think it is very clear what Pope Francis wants us to do, and this book is my attempt to humbly propose fifty-two ways to bring the vision of Pope Francis to the parish level. And, rather than offer more solutions that require rock-star pastors, large budgets, and an upper-middle-class demographic, I am offering exciting, practical, realistic, and doable strategies for transforming the way the average parish thinks, functions, worships, forms people in faith, and engages the world so that we can truly become a church on the move where people encounter the transforming grace of our Lord Jesus Christ.

Do we have a problem? Yes, oh, yes we do. However, with all due respect, I do believe this is going to be our finest hour!

A Note about St. Ignatius

You will notice in this book various mentions of St. Ignatius, the Society of Jesus that he founded (the Jesuits), and Ignatian spirituality. There are two reasons for this. One, I work for a Jesuit ministry, Loyola Press, and our charism—our particular ministry—is to develop books and teaching materials based in Ignatian spirituality. Two, our current pope is a Jesuit! Because he is pastor of the worldwide church, I have begun each chapter of this book with his words, which are inspiring, timely, and focused on the priorities of God's People—to be joyful and spiritually healthy and to reach out to all the world with God's love and Christ's salvation. Pope Francis speaks out consistently that we must become a church on the move. He speaks from his life experience and his holy calling, and both are informed by his Jesuit formation and the spiritual practices and principles developed by St. Ignatius.

Part One

How a Church on the Move Thinks

1

From Self-Sufficiency to Amazing Grace

Fearlessly proclaim the Gospel of hope, bringing the Lord's message into the brokenness of our time, tirelessly preaching forgiveness and the mercy of God.
—Pope Francis to the Bishops of Zimbabwe, February 6, 2014

The key to reviving any parish can be found in church basements all over the country.

And what, exactly, can be found in church basements? Twelve-step meetings. People do not go to twelve-step meetings because they like the music. They don't go because of how the space is decorated. They don't go because the seats are comfy. They don't go because the food is good. They go because they recognize that they are broken and that they cannot fix themselves through an act of their own will. They accept the fact that they need intervention.

Catholic parishes are in trouble because most folks today don't recognize their need to be saved and thus have little reason to squeeze churchgoing into their busy schedules. Bringing people to recognize their need to be saved is not the same as telling people that they are sinners. That kind of hellfire-and-brimstone preaching may have been effective at one time. Today, however, in the wake of serious moral failures on the part of leadership in the Catholic Church, the church is no longer in a position to point fingers at sinners and warn them of the dangers of hell.

For a parish to be effective today, it must focus on brokenness—the brokenness that is part of the human condition and that all of us share. For many, this brokenness is subtle: a sense of incompleteness, boredom, or restlessness. For others, it is dramatic: the collapse of life as it was once known. If the Catholic Church is to become a "church on the move," it must proclaim to the world that we all experience brokenness and that we are incapable of "fixing" ourselves.

It is no accident that the church's liturgical year begins with Advent, a season in which we focus on our need for an intervention. The prophets seek to bring us to the recognition that we are members of a dysfunctional human race in need of being saved. Contemporary thinking suggests that we can lift ourselves out of the mire of this dysfunction. While we as a human family can and should make progress, the very heart of Scripture's message is that even those efforts are tainted because our human wills are tainted. As with any dysfunctional family, the only solution must come from outside intervention, from someone who is not tainted by that particular family's dysfunction.

Jesus Christ is God's intervention. If a parish is going to be effective, everything it does must flow from this principle: we need to move from the illusion of self-sufficiency to the acceptance of God's intervention and the amazing grace we encounter through Jesus Christ.

Think about it: no one ever wrote a hymn about how he or she has been transformed by the remodeling of a sanctuary or by the coffee and donuts served in the parish hall after Mass. What we do have, however, in our treasury of hymns, is one of the most moving testimonies about human brokenness and the power of God's intervention:

Amazing grace! how sweet the sound
that saved a wretch like me!
I once was lost, but now am found,
was blind, but now I see.

I can think of a variety of ways that parishes can begin to move from an attitude of self-sufficiency to one of amazing grace. Here are just a few.

- Drop the flowery language in the parish mission statement about what a loving, caring, dedicated, and close-knit family the parish is, and replace it with a statement that describes the parish as a community of broken people who have found salvation in Jesus Christ and who invite others to do the same.
- Heighten focus on the Penitential Rite at Mass instead of rushing through it, enabling people to truly focus on their brokenness and to present it to the community and to the Lord. This can be done by slowing it down, adding silence, or adding melody.
- Have the parish pastoral council and parish staff work together to identify examples of brokenness and need in the community (loneliness, hunger, homelessness, broken relationships, unwanted pregnancies, anxiety and depression, illness and infirmity, poverty, unemployment) as well as what the parish is doing or might be able to do to address these needs. This list should be reviewed every so often to determine if there are new examples of brokenness in the community or new ideas for more effectively responding to existing needs.
- The name of Jesus should be spoken more often in all parish gatherings and in all parish communications, especially homilies. The only reason the parish exists is because of Jesus

Christ, and it is through his power alone that we are saved. We should be name-droppers! We Catholics often hide behind safe words and phrases such as "the church," or "our faith," or "the *Catechism*," instead of talking about Jesus as though he were in our midst—and he is.

- Parish bulletins should highlight stories of parishioners who have come to grips with their brokenness and are finding healing in Jesus Christ rather than just feature stories of award winners and parishioners who have achieved great goals. For those who wish to share their stories anonymously, that option should be available.

St. Ignatius of Loyola came to experience the power of Christ when his body and his life were literally "broken" by a cannonball. His painful experience, like that of St. Paul at his conversion, teaches all of us that the power of Christ enters in through the cracks of our own brokenness.

Few souls understand what God would accomplish in them if they were to abandon themselves unreservedly to Him and if they were to allow His grace to mold them accordingly.
—St. Ignatius of Loyola

Questions for Reflection and Discussion

- When did I come to recognize my own brokenness and my need for God's intervention?

- How is my parish presently focused on ministering to various forms of need and brokenness?

- What could my parish be doing to focus more effectively on people's brokenness? What examples of brokenness are most pressing in my community?

- How/where is God's amazing grace most evident in the life of my parish?

2

From Complacency to Urgency

I want a mess!
—Pope Francis to Argentine pilgrims in Brazil,
World Youth Day 2013

A friend of mine who works in diocesan ministry told me that he was asked to locate a church in the diocese that was big enough to handle an installation of a new auxiliary bishop. He did his research and found one suitable for such an occasion. When he contacted the parish to inquire about the possibility, however, he was told that there was an unavoidable conflict on that date at that time: weekly bingo.

I hope you're laughing at that, but only to keep from crying!

When bingo becomes a priority for followers of Jesus, something is wrong, and what's wrong is a lack of urgency in our approach to discipleship. The opposite of urgency is complacency. When we grow complacent, we lose our sense of focus, and we allow our priorities to get confused and disordered. We are anesthetized. Central to the gospel is a sense of urgency—not an anxious and fearful urgency but one that is colored by joy: why would we want to wait when God's grace is available to us right now? This is the urgency St. Paul expressed in his Second Letter to the Corinthians (6:2): "I tell you, now is the time of God's favor, now is the day of salvation."

A sense of urgency is a hallmark of success. Great leaders know how to create, instill, and sustain a sense of urgency in their followers. In his book *Leading Change*, leadership guru John P. Kotter explains that transformation is difficult in groups where complacency runs high and that complacency takes over when people don't recognize a visible crisis, have low expectations and narrow goals, are out of touch with those they are supposed to serve, and hear only "happy talk" from their leaders. Likewise, complacency is tidy, while urgency tends to be messy. No doubt this is what Pope Francis had in mind at World Youth Day in Brazil in 2013 when he encouraged Catholic youth to make a "mess."

In an effort to create a greater sense of urgency, many TV newscasts now introduce stories with graphics that blare "Breaking News!" or "Developing Story!" accompanied by sound effects (lots of *whoosh!* sounds) as one image and story gives way to the next. News, by its very nature, is supposed to create a sense of urgency; otherwise, it's not news. It is no accident, then, that the gospel we preach is called the Good *News!* This Good News is supposed to create a sense of urgency, something that Mark's Gospel captures by skipping all the preliminaries (genealogies and nativity stories) and beginning with an urgent announcement: "The beginning of the good news about Jesus the Messiah, the Son of God" (Mark 1:1). Just a few paragraphs later, Jesus appears on the scene, urgently announcing, "The time has come. The kingdom of God has come near. Repent and believe the good news!" (Mark 1:15). All that's missing is the *whoosh!* sound effect.

For Jesus, the time is now. It's always now. Complacency has no place in discipleship. And yet our parishes are often places of complacency. How can this complacency be dislodged? Here are a few suggestions.

- Nothing creates urgency like a crisis, and, while it is not our place to create false crises, it is our responsibility to help people recognize the crises that surround us and how, with God's grace, we can address them. Parishes need to focus more on addressing crises as opposed to offering feel-good experiences, what John Kotter refers to as "happy talk." (Ash Wednesday and the Lenten season, in particular, are two of the few times we seem to get this urgency right!)

- Pastors and other parish ministers can imitate Pope Francis by taking actions that have significant symbolic value. The pope moved out of the papal palace and gave up the luxury car. Are there extravagances in your parish that might be relinquished? Nothing speaks of complacency more powerfully than comfort, excess, and prosperity.

- Parishes need to set ministerial (not just financial) goals that raise the bar so that they cannot be achieved without cranking things up a notch, such as increasing the number of sick and infirm parishioners reached through ministry of care, meals served to the homeless, new parishioners welcomed, households contacted through evangelization efforts, and so on.

- Expectations need to be placed on parishioners. It is not enough to expect that they go to Mass and turn in an envelope. Parishes need to communicate consistently that it is the responsibility of the baptized to bring God's mercy to the world. (More on this in chapter 14.)

- The focus of the parish needs to turn outward as opposed to turning in on itself. The goal of the parish should be to transform the geographic region it resides in as opposed to being a "lodge" where people can escape from the world and daily living.

Without a sense of urgency, we can easily allow our attention to be diverted to trivial things. Ultimately, that is what the deadly sin of sloth is all about—paying attention to trivial things instead of to what is urgent for the health of our soul. Urgency need not mean that we act with speed, but rather, that we pay immediate attention to what deserves our undivided attention. In her book *The Preaching Life*, Barbara Brown Taylor explains that while God has given us the Good News and the grace to proclaim it, we also have the freedom to "lose our voices, to forget where we were going and why." She warns that if we do not bring our best efforts to proclaiming the gospel, the Christian church could very well be an exhibit in a museum someday.

Urgency is characteristic of the Holy Spirit, which is why Jesus said, according to more archaic translations, that "it is the Spirit which quickens" (John 6:63). This quickening refers to the first movement of a child in the mother's womb. For us, it refers to how the Holy Spirit stirs us to new life—calls us out of complacency—so that we may be present and alive right now to God's grace. May the Holy Spirit jar us and our parishes out of our complacency and quicken us so that we may live in the urgency of God's grace.

Pastoral ministry in a missionary key seeks to abandon the complacent attitude that says: "We have always done it this way." I invite everyone to be bold and creative in this task of rethinking the goals, structures, style and methods of evangelization in their respective communities.
—Pope Francis, *Evangelii Gaudium*, 33

Questions for Reflection and Discussion

- What are signs/indications of complacency in my own faith life?
- What are signs/indications of complacency in my parish/ faith community?
- Of the suggestions for dislodging complacency in a parish, which might be most effective or most needed in my parish?
- How has the Holy Spirit "quickened" me—stirred me to new life?

3

From Cynicism to Hope

Today . . . amid so much darkness, we need to see the light of
hope and to be men and women who bring hope to others.
—Pope Francis at his Inaugural Mass, March 19, 2013

Energetic music and singing are a big part of spectator sports. As long as music and singing are present, there's hope for your team. When the singing stops, it's a sure sign that hope has evaporated, and when hope evaporates, cynicism—characterized by grumbling or murmuring—takes over. "Why'd they leave him in the game so long? His arm is obviously tired." "Oh c'mon! My grandmother can skate faster than that!" "I never liked this quarterback anyway!"

This relationship between music/singing and hope is captured in Scripture. When the Jewish people are led from slavery in Egypt to freedom, they immediately burst into song: "I will sing to the Lord, for he is highly exalted. Both horse and driver he has hurled into the sea" (Exodus 15:1). Hope springs eternal. Well, not exactly eternal. Just several verses later, the singing stops, and the grumbling begins as the people grow hot, tired, and thirsty: "If only we had died by the Lord's hand in Egypt! There we sat around pots of meat and ate all the food we wanted, but you have brought us out into this desert to starve this entire assembly to death" (Exodus 16:3). While grumbling in difficult situations is human nature and may seem harmless,

Moses warns that it masks the real question: "Is the Lord among us or not?" (Exodus 17:7). Several centuries later, when the people of Israel find themselves in exile in Babylon, their lack of hope is characterized by their inability to sing.

> By the rivers of Babylon we sat and wept
>> when we remembered Zion.
> There on the poplars
>> we hung our harps,
> for there our captors asked us for songs,
>> our tormentors demanded songs of joy;
>> they said, "Sing us one of the songs of Zion!"
> How can we sing the songs of the Lord
>> while in a foreign land? (Psalm 137:1–4)

On the flip side, Scripture frequently alludes to music and singing as an important expression of faith and hope.

- More than a dozen psalms encourage us to "sing to the Lord."
- Jesus and the apostles sang at the Last Supper before Jesus experienced his agony in the garden. (Matthew 26:30)
- St. Paul, along with his companion Silas, sang songs while in prison (Acts 16:25), encouraged the Ephesians to address one another "with psalms, hymns, and songs from the Spirit. Sing and make music from your heart to the Lord" (Ephesians 5:19), and encouraged the Colossians to "teach and admonish one another with all wisdom through psalms, hymns, and songs from the Spirit, singing to God with gratitude in your hearts" (Colossians 3:16).

When singing is absent, it is often replaced by grumbling, which is more than happy to fill the vacuum. In a homily, Pope Francis referred to the experience of the two disciples on the road to Emmaus to warn of how grumbling dashes hope:

They were afraid. All of the disciples were afraid. And the more they complained, the more they were closed in on themselves: they did not have a horizon before them, only a wall. And they stewed, so to speak, their lives in the juice of their complaints and kept going on and on and on with the complaining. I think that many times when difficult things happen, including when we are visited by the cross, we run the risk of closing ourselves off in complaints.

In his apostolic letter *Evangelii Gaudium*, Pope Francis laments the constant bickering, grumbling, and complaining that take place within the church itself. A church on the move cannot be weighed down by grumbling, because the more we grumble, the more we are asking, "Is God in our midst or not?" So what do I propose as an antidote to grumbling? Singing! A church on the move must not be a church without song! I propose that every parish gathering, every meeting, and especially every catechetical session include singing, whether it be a hymn, a chant, or just a refrain. Without song, we are like a people in exile, a people without hope. Such hopelessness once led Friedrich Nietzsche to say, "The world no longer believes because believers no longer sing." Are there things to complain and grumble about? Of course! However, faith and hope adamantly refuse to believe that the world cannot become a better place.

I was struck by the power of singing while on pilgrimage to Spain and Rome. I observed a group of pilgrims in Ávila, Spain, gathered in the town square joyfully singing hymns of praise while clapping their hands. Later when our group returned to our bus, I lamented to my friend and colleague Tom McGrath that our group had not done any singing on our pilgrimage. We committed ourselves to changing that. We put our heads together and identified a number of songs and refrains that can be easily sung without hymnals or worship aids. From that point on, each time our group gathered for prayer and liturgy, we led the group in sung refrains that raised the level of joy on our pilgrimage.

How hard would it be for every parish and faith community to identify ten to twelve go-to hymns and refrains that could be sung spontaneously at any parish gathering? The songs should be short, snappy, uplifting, and easy to learn and sing. One person from every parish organization could be appointed to initiate singing whenever that particular group gathers.

Whenever followers of Jesus gather, before we can be sucked into the temptation to grumble, we should raise our voices in song and unleash the hope that is at the very core of the gospel message. St. Teresa of Ávila (who lived in the very place where I witnessed such joyful singing on my pilgrimage!) said to let the presence of God "settle into your bones, and allow your soul the freedom to sing, dance, praise, and love." If God is in our midst, we should be singing. And if we are singing, perhaps we won't be so quick to grumble. And if we're not grumbling, perhaps others will recognize that God is in our midst. And perhaps then we can become a church on the move.

I find that prayer and song can take me beyond the pain.
—Sister Thea Bowman, reflecting on the power of song to help her cope with cancer

Questions for Reflection and Discussion

- What do I find myself grumbling about the most?
- Whom do I know who does the least amount of grumbling?
- How are music and singing related to hope?
- What ten songs, hymns, or refrains would I select as my go-to hymns for my parish or faith community to sing at any parish gathering?

4

From Fog to Vision

I see the church as a field hospital after battle.
—Pope Francis, interview with *America* magazine,
September 19, 2013

Before the invention of the GPS, giving directions was an art form;
it required the person giving directions to "paint a picture" for the
person who would be navigating. Rather than simply saying, "Drive
four miles and then turn left on Route 83," folks gave directions
in a more folksy manner: "After you pass the hot-dog stand with
the giant hot dog on the roof, look for a huge yellow house with
blue shutters on the right; make a left there, and then look for the
water tower. . . ." Sure, it was less scientific, but it was much more
imaginative!

The most effective leaders know how to "paint a picture," or articulate a vision of the future: a hoped-for reality. With divine imagination, Jesus laid out a vision that is ambitious and lofty enough to
have inspired followers for more than two thousand years to move
according to his directions. To be a church on the move is to be a
church that moves according to the vision of Jesus Christ. Unfortunately, as a church we too often find ourselves navigating through
the fog of our own agendas and ideologies, unable to see clearly
the vision that Jesus has laid out for us. Our parishes too often

plod along, doing what we've been doing for so many years because that's what we do, while people are wondering just what it is that we do. For starters, we need to recapture the "communicability" of Jesus' vision. Pope Francis has proved to be a master of this skill. In an interview with *America* magazine (Sept. 19, 2013), Pope Francis articulated his vision—painted a picture—for the church in under one hundred words:

> The thing the church needs most today is the ability to heal wounds and to warm the hearts of the faithful; it needs nearness, proximity. I see the church as a field hospital after battle. It is useless to ask a seriously injured person if he has high cholesterol and about the level of his blood sugars! You have to heal his wounds. Then we can talk about everything else. Heal the wounds, heal the wounds. . . . And you have to start from the ground up.

The responsibility for promulgating this vision at the parish level falls primarily to the pastor. Interestingly enough, and unfortunately, pastors tend to articulate a vision primarily when finances are involved. The result of this for the average parishioner is that the response—the way we embrace and participate in that vision—is through giving money. In fact, many such capital campaigns, during which the pastor speaks at all the Masses, culminate in providing parishioners with pledge cards that they are to fill out and return as a way of showing their participation in the mission of the parish. These pledge cards are often steeped in language that reflects the vision of the parish and the church as a whole, but the bottom line is that the parishioner's response is primarily financial. When it comes to a vision for the church, and especially for the parish, we rarely ask churchgoers to truly embrace the vision and incorporate it into their lives.

A church on the move needs to have *parishioners* who are doing the heavy lifting. To achieve that, I would like to propose a different kind of pledge card: a "Discipleship Pledge Card." At a specific time of the year (whenever it would be most productive for a particular parish), the pastor or some designated speaker should speak at all the Masses about what it means to be a disciple of Christ, articulating the vision for the parish and the church. Parishioners can then be given a pledge card inviting them to reflect on, and then state, how they plan to do the following:

- deepen their relationship with Christ (prayer)
- deepen their knowledge of Christ (study)
- share their gifts with others (generosity/stewardship)
- reach out to others (evangelization)

Just as we often provide various models of giving when it comes to financial pledge cards, the Discipleship Pledge Cards (and the inspirational talks at Mass) should provide people with concrete options for how to strengthen their life of prayer, study, generosity, and evangelization (with an emphasis on opportunities in the home and at work). Here are some examples.

Prayer (I will commit to . . .)

- using the 3-Minute Retreat, Sacred Space, Give Us This Day, or other apps/online/print resources for daily prayer.
- spending thirty minutes each week in the Adoration chapel.
- praying the rosary daily and/or praying with my family.
- praying the daily *examen* each morning and evening on the train.

Study (I will commit to . . .)

- using resources recommended by the parish to to get background on the Sunday Scripture readings each week.

- participating in a parish book club to read inspirational Catholic literature.
- attending the parish Scripture study or other adult faith-formation opportunity.
- participating in a small faith group organized by the parish.

Generosity (I will commit to . . .)

- spending more time helping my kids with their homework.
- volunteering to work at (or donate to) the food pantry once per month.
- assisting as a catechist or catechist aide.
- becoming a Minister of Care to bring Holy Communion to the sick and homebound.

Evangelization (I will commit to . . .)

- talking to my kids/family about my faith.
- sharing with others Catholic books, DVDs, CDs I've read or watched or listened to.
- using social media to make references to my Catholic faith.
- inviting friends to parish functions and especially to Mass, prayer experiences/devotions, and learning experiences.

A church on the move needs to provide people with concrete ways to embrace the vision of Christ and to actively participate in his mission. It's easy to contribute financially and leave the work to others, but the faith community thrives and grows when all participate.

If you want to build a ship, don't drum up people to collect wood and don't assign them tasks and work, but rather teach them to long for the endless immensity of the sea.
—Antoine de Saint-Exupéry

Questions for Reflection and Discussion

- Who is a leader I respect who paints a picture for others to follow?

- If I were to articulate to someone a vision for my life of faith and discipleship, what would I say?

- What am I presently doing to deepen my relationship with Jesus? What specifically am I doing in the areas of prayer, study, generosity, and evangelization?

- What other suggestions would I add to the lists above to give people concrete examples of how to put their commitment into action?

5

From Superficial Happiness to Authentic Joy

I realize, of course, that joy is not expressed the same way at all times in life, especially at moments of great difficulty. Joy adapts and changes, but it always endures, even as a flicker of light born of our personal certainty that, when everything is said and done, we are infinitely loved.
—Pope Francis, *Evangelii Gaudium*

Back in the day, two of the most beloved characters on TV were Aunt Bee (*The Andy Griffith Show*) and Jim Anderson (*Father Knows Best*). Both characters were warm and fuzzy, always smiling, always loving, always kindhearted. It turns out, however, that the actors who played these roles were, in real life, nothing like the characters they portrayed. Frances Bavier, who portrayed the kindly Aunt Bee who lovingly cared for Andy and Opie, was, according to some reports, a cantankerous woman with a short fuse. Likewise, Robert Young, who played the ever-patient and seemingly carefree dad, Jim Anderson, on *Father Knows Best* (and later the affable and sensitive Dr. Marcus Welby), struggled with depression and alcoholism in real life.

One of the problems we face in striving to present our church as a church on the move is that we often think that it's necessary to put on a persona when doing the Lord's work, as if we need to become Aunt Bee or Jim Anderson—kindly, affable, gentle, carefree, and seemingly perfect people. Otherwise known as phony.

Now, before we talk about moving from superficial happiness to authentic joy, we need to grapple with the reality that Catholics are not known for being joyous or happy, superficially or any other way. Quite the contrary: we have an image of being dour. Billy Joel famously sang that he'd rather laugh with the sinners than cry with the saints, because sinners have much more fun. Part of that is our depiction of the saints, many of whom were martyrs, so they don't appear to be having too much fun. Another part of that is the centuries-long European influence on Catholicism, which always seemed suspicious of too much emotion. Finally, if you flip through channels on a Sunday morning, you will no doubt discover that Catholic broadcasting is far more subdued—often almost sedate—compared to the broadcasts of non-Catholic worship services.

In an effort to correct this, many Catholics are promoting what they refer to as "evangelical Catholicism." I fully get this concept and, for the most part, agree with it. However it has given birth to what I refer to as the "hipster Catholic." In an effort to overcome this dour reputation, some Catholic personalities have overcompensated, presenting themselves as incredibly extroverted, consistently upbeat, always jovial, and perpetually fired up. We find such personas on the speaking circuit (especially for youth ministry) and in inspirational videos. They are sending the unmistakable message that this is what it looks like to be on fire for Christ. The only problem is, half the Catholic population is comprised of introverts who simply cannot replicate this approach. We must not allow the New Evangelization to be confused with some form of "new extroversion" that is judged by its loudness. If we do so, we risk looking and sounding like the long line of televangelists whose superficiality came to be recognized as the snake oil it truly was.

For those who are extroverts, showing joy can be quite natural. They can smile, laugh, and speak with excitement with great ease. For the fifty percent of the church who are introverts—and I include myself in that group (yes, public speakers can also be introverts!)—displaying such affect can feel very phony. It is important to remember that the joy we show must be authentic. We need not be loud to express joy. Our smiles need not be ear to ear. Our laughing need not reach high decibels. We can and must, however, find quiet and authentic ways of sharing our joy with others.

Catholic evangelism needs to develop its own style, and we can begin by differentiating between happiness and joy. We do a disservice to the gospel when we reduce joy to happiness. The two are not equivalent. Happiness is a fleeting emotion that comes and goes and is controlled by external factors. A church on the move is not one that simply paints on a smiley face and sings "Don't worry, be happy!" A church on the move does not look at the world through rose-colored glasses. Rather, a church on the move is one that embodies joy, a deep-down gladness that cannot be taken away from us, even in the midst of pain and suffering. It is not possible to be happy and sad at the same time. It is possible, however, to carry joy in the midst of sadness.

So how does a church on the move share joy? We do so by offering our presence to others, especially to those overwhelmed by brokenness. Ignatian spirituality compels us to seek out others with whom to share the journey. Every parish should ask itself, "Who are we present to? Who most needs our presence?" We don't try to erase their sadness. We don't try to wipe away their tears. We are simply present to them in the moment. We don't glibly tell people who are sad to smile and forget all their worries. As people who embody the joy of the Resurrection, we make ourselves present to them, holding the joy of the risen Christ within us until such time as those who are grieving are ready once again to embrace it. People who are not capable of experiencing joy at a particular moment in life do not want others flaunting joy in their face. They do, however, want and need to be reminded that joy is within reach.

To be a church on the move, we need to identify those places and experiences in life where joy is lacking and commit to being present there. We are called to be consistent and authentic in all our encounters with others. A church on the move is a church that brings an authentic joy to the world, especially in those places where joy is seemingly out of reach.

For me, prayer is a surge of the heart, it is a simple look turned toward heaven, it is a cry of recognition and of love, embracing both trial and joy.
—St. Thérèse of Lisieux

Questions for Reflection and Discussion

- Am I an introvert or an extrovert? How easy or difficult is it for me to share joy with others?
- What people in my life share joy with me? How do they do it? How do I share joy with others?
- Was there a time when I could not experience joy but knew it was within reach because of someone else's presence?
- In my community, who is experiencing the absence of joy? Is my parish present to them? How can my parish increase its presence to others so that they might know that joy is within reach?

6

From Calendar, Fiscal, or Academic Year to Liturgical Year

If Christ were not raised, Christianity would lose its very meaning; the whole mission of the Church would lose its impulse, for this is the point from which it first set out and continues to set out ever anew.

—Pope Francis, *Urbi et Orbi* message, April 20, 2014

With all the traveling I do, sometimes my calendar can get a little crazy. I've gotten better at managing it, but on more than one occasion I have found myself looking at my overbooked calendar and asking, "What was I thinking when I said yes to all these things?" In the midst of busyness, I can sometimes fail to look ahead and recognize significant events in my life and create a buffer zone around them so that I can be truly present for something that means a lot to me, such as an important birthday or a wedding anniversary.

In parish life, we often overbook. Even when we have "calendaring" meetings that should, theoretically, remove any conflicts, we still find ourselves overbooked and unable to devote time and energy to those things that are most important to us as a faith community—such as celebrating the death and resurrection of Jesus! As a result, it is not uncommon to see parishes promoting a comedy night or a fashion show or a March Madness/Final Four party during the season of Lent, our most solemn time of the year! Apparently, since these events always happened at that time of the year, no one questioned whether that was the best time to invest energy in such activities.

A church on the move should not be confused with a church that has a lot of moving parts. Busy parishes can create a perception of health just by the number of activities packing the calendar. However, just as it is possible for an individual to be a workaholic and yet be guilty of sloth (inattention to one's spiritual well-being), a parish can be extremely busy and yet be slothful. A church that is truly on the move needs to have a laser-sharp focus on its priorities.

The truth is, when parishes suffer from an overcrowded calendar, it is not a problem of time management, per se. In fact, the late author and speaker Stephen Covey insisted that there was no such thing as time management. What he advocated was self-management. If we manage ourselves and our priorities properly, our time will end up being better managed. Covey was noted for recommending a self-management matrix or grid that consisted of four quadrants arranged by *importance* (activities that lead to achieving your goals) and *urgency* (activities that demand immediate attention but are often linked to achieving someone else's goals).

1 High Importance/High Urgency	2 High Importance/Low Urgency
3 Low Importance/High Urgency	4 Low Importance/Low Urgency

A church on the move needs to spend less time in Quadrant 3, focused on events that eat up lots of time and energy without advancing the mission of Jesus Christ, and instead spend increasing amounts of time in Quadrant 2, focusing on those things that are of the utmost importance to the mission of the church but not necessarily urgent (time sensitive)—and nothing is more important to the mission of the church than evangelization. In fact, Pope Paul VI stated unequivocally that "the church exists in order to evangelize" (*Evangelii Nuntiandi*). Simply put, our mission is to lead people to conversion—transformation of hearts and minds—through the death and resurrection of Jesus Christ. In practical terms, this means that celebrating the death and resurrection of Jesus Christ must be central to the planning and calendaring of *all* parish events. That means that we don't begin planning with the first day of the calendar year (January 1), the first day of the fiscal year (whatever that date may be for your parish/diocese), or the first day of the academic year (near or on September 1). Rather, parish planning and calendaring should center on the Liturgical calendar, which focuses on the paschal mystery of Jesus Christ, with the Triduum at its center.

Before anything else in the life of the parish is planned or calendared, the dates for the Triduum, Easter (and its fifty days), Holy Week, Lent, and Ash Wednesday should be noted, highlighted, and etched in stone. From there, the parish must plan and calendar how these seasons and feasts will be observed appropriately. Lenten programs, the Lenten mission, penance and reconciliation services, RCIA rites, and sacramental celebrations during the Easter season are just some of the things that must be given priority.

Everything else the parish does, week in and week out, is directed toward the celebration of the death and resurrection of Jesus, with each Sunday of the liturgical calendar being a "mini-Easter." Once this is all in place, parishes can determine which activities truly support the parish mission and what time of year is most appropriate for these activities. Each ministry and organization in the parish should be directed to do its own planning with the Triduum/Easter in mind

and to come to the table ready to show how its calendaring propos-
als observe this and further the mission of the parish. Perhaps the
comedy night or the fashion show, which has always taken place in
March, can take place at a time of year other than Lent (if at all),
because they don't contribute to (and in some ways may be in conflict with) the parish's observance of that season or the overall parish
mission.

A parish I used to belong to often bragged about how vibrant it
was, based on its activity calendar. On any given day, people were
coming and going in the parish: picking up Market Day orders,
dropping off kids for volleyball practice, attending their kids' basketball tournament, attending moms'-club meetings to plan the fashion
show or men's-club meetings to plan the Final Four party, playing in
the over-thirty basketball league, and so on. Little of it, however, had
to do with Jesus Christ and transforming hearts and minds through
his death and resurrection. And this was reflected most on Sundays
when the majority of those people zipping in and out of the parish
during the week were nowhere to be found at Mass. It was a parish
with lots of moving parts, but it was not a church on the move. For
that to happen, we must be a church powered by the death and resurrection of Jesus!

———————————

*Therefore the Easter triduum of the passion and resurrection of
Christ is the culmination of the entire liturgical year. Thus the
solemnity of Easter has the same kind of preeminence in the
liturgical year that Sunday has in the week.*
—*General Instruction of the Roman Missal*, 18

Questions for Reflection and Discussion

- What causes my own personal calendar to get away from me sometimes?
- To what extent is the Triduum/Easter acknowledged as the center of my parish's life?
- In which of the four quadrants described above is my parish spending most of its time? And what activities are in that quadrant?
- What can my parish do to spend more time in Quadrant 2, paying attention to things that are of high importance but not necessarily urgent?

7

From a Learned Faith to a Lived Faith

If our missionary efforts are to bear fruit, the example of the "hidden Christians" has much to teach us. Though small in number and daily facing persecution, these believers were able to preserve the faith by being attentive to their personal relationship with Jesus, a relationship built on a solid prayer life and a sincere commitment to the welfare of the community.
—Pope Francis to Japanese Bishops about Japan's "Hidden Christians," March 20, 2015

When I was in parish ministry on the far southeast side of Chicago many years ago, there was a very real possibility that we would not get a resident pastor after our present pastor moved on. I was told by many that there was a good chance I would be appointed pastoral coordinator, facilitating the daily life of the parish in the absence of a resident pastor. In speaking with parishioners, however, I discovered that there was a palpable fear of not having a resident pastor, as though it would spell the death of the parish. As excited as I was about the possibility of serving as a pastoral coordinator, I approached a priest who had previously served in the parish as an associate and encouraged him to apply for the pastorate. He did so and was appointed pastor, much to the initial joy and relief of many parishioners. The joy and relief were short-lived, however, as the new pastor's lack of leadership skills became quickly evident. Within a year, he let me go as pastoral associate, and within two more years he resigned as pastor, and the parish went into a free fall. Despite the appointment of another pastor, within ten years the parish was closed.

Contrast that with the experience of the Catholic Church in Japan. Despite successful efforts by Jesuit missionaries, led by St. Francis Xavier, which resulted in a flourishing Catholic community of more than 100,000 converts, Christianity was eventually repressed by the prevailing government. Many leaders, including St. Paul Miki and his companions, were martyred, and the Catholic community went underground, becoming known as the "hidden Christians." Over the next 250 years, the hidden Christians, without priests, maintained elements of their faith, practicing in secret. When Japanese isolation ended in 1853 and the country once again engaged in trade and contact with the world, Christian missionaries arrived and were astonished to meet a small group of elderly peasants representing a community that had retained elements of Catholicism for two and a half centuries, maintained only by the domestic church.

Good pastoring is crucial to the life of the church, but faith is (or should be) primarily fed and nourished in the home. The success of a parish, therefore, is not to be measured by the level of activity taking place on parish grounds, but rather by the extent to which the Catholic faith is being lived and practiced in homes, in the community, and in the world. If a parish is to succeed and be part of a church on the move, pastoral leadership needs to shift from hosting Catholic programs that occur solely "on campus" to supporting Catholic practices that take place daily in homes, at work, at school, and in the community—practices that help people learn to "find

God in all things," a phrase at the heart of Ignatian spirituality lived out so powerfully by those Jesuits in Japan. Some practices might be:

- wearing medals, crosses, and scapulars
- praying the rosary and novenas
- fasting, abstaining from meat
- blessing ourselves and others
- observing the liturgical calendar
- practicing stewardship and solidarity
- praying with Mary and the communion of saints
- praying the Liturgy of the Hours
- performing corporal and spiritual works of mercy
- working for social justice
- practicing virtues
- going on pilgrimages
- venerating relics
- reading and praying Scripture
- reading Catholic literature
- learning traditional prayers
- singing/listening to hymns
- going on retreat

These are practices that take place in the home and in the public square on the other six days of the week, when most of us are not in church but in the world. To be a church on the move, we need to teach these practices so that we Catholics can maintain our way of life and can do so even if forced to live "underground," as the "hidden Christians" in Japan once did. One effective way of doing this is through mentoring, which is not to be confused with tutoring. When we tutor, we are helping someone learn concepts and ideas. When we mentor, we are helping someone learn attitudes, values, and behaviors. I suggest implementing mentoring relationships for Catholic practices in the following settings:

- RCIA sponsors with catechumens and candidates
- confirmation sponsors with those being confirmed
- young adults with teens in the youth group
- older married couples with newly married couples (part of marriage prep)
- older parents with new parents (part of baptismal prep)
- older students with younger students (in a school or religious education setting)

(For more information about fostering mentoring relationships related to Catholic practices, see http://www.loyolapress.com/assets/trade/practice-makes-catholic--leader-guide.pdf.)

The goal of a parish is not to get more people in the pews but to get the people who are in the pews to go forth and transform the world. The purpose of going to church is to be nourished and equipped to go forth—to be sent—which is why we call our Catholic worship the Mass: it comes from the Latin word *missa*, which means "sent." Let's be sure that we are sending Catholics into the world fully equipped with practices that enable them to be transformed and to transform the world they engage.

If you don't behave as you believe, you will end up believing as you behave.
—attributed to Archbishop Fulton J. Sheen

Questions for Reflection and Discussion

- In what ways do our Catholic parishes rely too heavily on the pastor and staff? How true is this in my parish?
- In what ways are Catholic practices being taught in my parish faith community?
- Whom do I know who practices their Catholic faith every day of the week?
- What lesson can we learn from the "hidden Christians" of Japan?

8

From Religion to Spirituality

There is also a "spiritual Alzheimer's disease" . . . losing the memory of our personal . . . history with the Lord and our "first love." It involves a progressive decline in the spiritual faculties, which . . . greatly handicaps a person.
—Pope Francis, address to the Curia, December 22, 2014

On my way to work each day, as I ride the train from the south side to the north side of Chicago, I see a variety of storefronts advertising spiritual wellness—places that supposedly nurture one's body, mind, and spirit in order to achieve serenity and calmness, as well as answers to life's questions, through various programs and classes. The major emphasis is that these centers are inclusive, nonjudgmental, and accepting, meaning that they are not tied to a denomination or religion. They cater to folks who describe themselves as "spiritual but not religious." At the same time, it doesn't take a rocket scientist to conclude that many of their offerings are drawn from various traditions, primarily Hinduism, Buddhism, and the ancient wisdom of kabbalah, which has its origins in Judaism. The message is clear: these faith traditions are viewed as spiritual paths.

Most people don't see Catholicism that way; they see it as an institution. Many people, including many Catholics, would not describe Catholicism as a spiritual path. And that's unfortunate in a world where more and more people are calling themselves spiritual but not religious. In order for the Catholic Church to become a church on the move, we need to emphasize that Catholicism *is* a spiritual path, not just a set of doctrines and laws to abide by. So, what would it look like if a Catholic parish rented a storefront and advertised "spiritual wellness"? What could the church offer? What might the "menu" of offerings look like? Here's a sample.

- **Daily *examen*:** a quick (twenty minutes), easy, contemplative daily practice to recognize God more clearly in your daily living

- **Guided meditation:** twenty-, thirty- or forty-minute sessions of guided reflection to get in touch with God's will for your life

- **Centering prayer:** a type of silent prayer designed to help the person experience God's presence and overcome distractions

- **The Spiritual Exercises:** a compilation of meditations, prayers, and contemplative practices developed by St. Ignatius of Loyola to deepen one's relationship with God

- **Taizé prayer:** a prayer form utilizing music that is chant-like and accompanied by Scripture and silent meditation

- **Adoration of the Blessed Sacrament:** an experience of silence in the presence of Jesus

- **Lectio divina:** an experience of sacred reading and meditation on brief Scripture passages

- **Spiritual direction:** an opportunity to meet regularly with another person to discover and talk about God's presence and action in everyday life

- **Rosary:** a form of meditation using prayer beads and the repetition of sacred verses inspired by Scripture to dwell on the mysteries of God's revealed presence in Jesus

- **Liturgy of the Hours:** a method of prayer to make sacred the various times of the day—morning, afternoon, evening, night
- **Way of the Cross:** a meditative walk through Jesus' journey to the cross and his resurrection
- **Spiritual discernment:** a process for recognizing God's will for your life at moments of transition and crisis
- **Days of reflection:** a daylong experience of reflecting on your life in light of Scripture and Tradition

That's only the tip of the iceberg, but you get the idea. You might say that it sounds like the kinds of offerings one might find at a Catholic retreat house. Precisely! But when did we decide as a church to relegate such offerings to retreat houses? If we are going to be a church on the move, it is imperative that our parishes become spiritual wellness centers, not just activity centers. And if you are thinking that this is just offering touchy-feely stuff that helps some people feel good about themselves, I might point out that, according to research done by the Gallup Organization, one of the most important factors in determining a church's health is the extent to which members feel that their spiritual needs are being met (*Growing an Engaged Church*, Albert L. Winseman, Gallup Press). Likewise, it is important to remember that while the Eucharist is central to our spiritual lives as Catholics, it is not the only way that one can encounter spiritual enrichment. The Eucharist is the "summit" of our spiritual lives, and any summit is reached by climbing steps along the way.

What does it take for a parish to move toward becoming a spiritual wellness center? Does it require that every parish hire a professional retreat master and spiritual director? While that would be nice, parish budgets are already stretched. Instead, I suggest that parishes recruit and train a number of parishioners one at a time to facilitate various spiritual enrichment opportunities. At Loyola Press, where I work, I'm amazed at the number of young coworkers—editors, designers, project managers—who also work part-time as yoga instructors, spin-class leaders, and aerobics trainers. Their contemporaries are trusting them to lead them through activities that will bring about physical and emotional wellness. We should be recruiting these same young people and forming/training them to lead activities, such as the ones listed above, that foster spiritual wellness. Obviously, some roles, such as spiritual director, require formal training. What's stopping us from sending parishioners to get training in spiritual direction in the same way that we send parishioners for lay-ministry formation or the diaconate? To be a spiritual director (or perhaps, less intimidating, a spiritual companion), an advanced degree is not required. What is needed is some basic formation in spirituality and a supervised internship. Information about such training and formation programs necessary for becoming a spiritual director can be found on the Web site for Spiritual Directors International.

A church on the move must not settle for being an activity center. While we may be able to attract a number of people through a variety of fun and engaging activities, we are called to bring people into a deeper relationship with God. We are called to be spiritual wellness centers.

———————

As strolling, walking and running are bodily exercises, so every way of preparing and disposing the soul to rid itself of all the disordered tendencies, and, after it is rid, to seek and find the Divine Will as to the management of one's life for the salvation of the soul, is called a Spiritual Exercise.
—St. Ignatius of Loyola, First Annotation, *The Spiritual Exercises*

Questions for Reflection and Discussion

- What do I do to maintain and foster my own spiritual wellness?
- What would I like to see my parish do to foster spiritual wellness?
- What activity(ies) do I find most attractive in the "menu" for spiritual wellness that is included earlier in this chapter? What would I add?
- If I were called to facilitate others in a spiritual wellness activity, what might that activity be?

9

From Aiming to Please to Remaining True to Our Identity

It is undeniable that many people feel disillusioned and no longer identify with the Catholic tradition.
—Pope Francis, *Evangelii Gaudium*, 70

Between 2012 and 2014, retail giant JCPenney nearly ran itself out of business. A new CEO with an impressive record of previous successes took over in November of 2011, and within months he announced major changes that emulated the success of other major corporations. There were to be fewer promotions, replaced by everyday low prices and, in place of one big store, each JCPenney store would be composed of smaller shops, or boutiques. A brand-new JCPenney logo—the third in three years—was unveiled. The result of all of these changes was that JCPenney's customers left in droves and headed for Macy's. What went wrong? All the things that JCPenney attempted to put in place were being done successfully elsewhere. The problem was that the changes resulted in a store that no longer felt like JCPenney. In an effort to please everybody, the retail giant accomplished the exact opposite and completely lost its own identity and brand.

Today, too many pastoral leaders of Catholic parishes are making the same mistake. They are attending workshops and seminars held by leaders and pastors of megachurches—some Catholic, some Protestant—and are returning with a laundry list of ideas (that do not necessarily reflect and reinforce Catholic identity) to breathe new life into their faltering parishes. When they observe these megachurches in action, here's what they see:

- jumbo video screens and high-tech media in the worship spaces
- upbeat contemporary concert-like music
- cafes, coffeehouses, and food courts
- dramatized Scripture presentations
- rock-climbing walls and gymnasiums
- bookstores and gift shops
- self-improvement workshops and seminars

Now the last thing I want to sound like is a curmudgeon, saying something like, "We didn't have any of these gizmos and shenanigans when I was young, and people were flocking to church!" The truth is, some of these innovations are proving to be quite effective at various churches, Protestant and Catholic alike. The temptation we need to avoid is to forge ahead making these changes without knowing how they will reinforce our core identity. Superficial changes will not solve the critical issues we face as a church, not the least of which is our seeming inability to inspire people to become disciples of Christ. In fact, many millennials are telling us that they are turned off by efforts that churches are making to be "with it." In a *Washington Post* opinion piece (April 30, 2015), Rachel Held Evans emphasized that the types of innovations mentioned above, while not bad ideas in and of themselves, will not solve the problem of drawing millennials back to church. She asserts that young people do not want to be entertained and that, in fact, over two-thirds of them prefer a more classic approach rather than a trendier one. What they are looking for is authenticity and inclusivity.

So, before your parish invests in a jumbo video screen and hires a rock musician to redesign and direct the parish music program, take a serious look at how your parish is offering an experience of God. And it's not enough to say that "we offer the Mass and sacraments," even though those realities are at the core of who we are and what we do. If we are to avoid the mistakes that JCPenney made, we need to be more attentive to our core identity and build on our strengths, making sure that any innovations we pursue flow from and reinforce these strengths. And just what constitutes the core identity of any Catholic faith community? In my book *Practice Makes Catholic: Moving from a Learned Faith to a Lived Faith*, I identify five core characteristics of Catholic identity. I offer them here in the form of questions that I propose every parish staff and pastoral council reflect on before moving forward on some innovation.

- **A Sense of the Sacred (sacramentality).** Recognizing that the most important things in life are intangible (love, acceptance, belonging, forgiveness, commitment), how will this innovation help people "speak" a language of mystery that transcends words and instead relies on signs, symbolic actions and objects, rituals, and gestures?

- **A Commitment to Community.** Recognizing that all people are created in the image and likeness of a Trinitarian God (a loving community of Persons), how will this innovation enhance a true communal experience that challenges the rampant individualism of our society?

- **A Respect for Human Life and Commitment to Social Justice.** Recognizing that each human being possesses dignity, how will this innovation invite or challenge people to show a profound respect for all human life, from the moment of conception to the moment of natural death and beyond? How will this innovation invite or challenge people to work to support structures and practices in society that respect the dignity of human beings?

- **A Reverence for Scripture and Tradition.** Recognizing that God has revealed all that we need to know in order to enter into relationship with him and all his children, how will this innovation help people to revere God's revelation in Scripture and Tradition and view it as a living, breathing Word that guides and sustains us?

- **A Disposition of Faith and Hope and Not Despair.** Recognizing that God has drawn near to us through his Son, Jesus Christ, how will this innovation help people bring hope to others?

Willow Creek Church (South Barrington, Illinois), Saddleback Church (Lake Forest, California), Church of the Nativity (Baltimore, Maryland), and Old St. Patrick's Church (Chicago, Illinois) may be extraordinary examples of churches doing an amazing job of making disciples of Jesus Christ. This does not mean that each parish should go out and automatically adopt all the innovations these communities have implemented. To do so is to risk going down the same road that led to the near-ruin of JCPenney. Rather, each parish should look closely at how it is embodying its core Catholic identity and then seek ways to strengthen that core identity. That may mean purchasing a high-tech jumbo video screen for the sanctuary. Then again, it may not. But it does mean becoming a church on the move.

Beneath all changes there are many realities which do not change, and which have their ultimate foundation in Christ, Who is the same yesterday and today, yes and forever.
— *Gaudium et Spes*, 10

Questions for Reflection and Discussion

- What innovations have I seen in parishes/churches that risk coming across as slick or trendy?
- How can my parish/faith community better foster a sense of Catholic identity?
- What innovations might create more interest in the Catholic faith among millennials while remaining true to the core principles of Catholic identity?

Part Two

How a Church on the Move Functions

10

From (We Hope!) Benevolent Dictatorship and Fiat to Collaboration and Consensus

---

We should not even think, therefore, that "thinking with the church" means only thinking with the hierarchy of the church.
—Pope Francis, interview with *America* magazine, October 2013

When I was working in parish ministry, the pastor indicated that he wanted to reduce the number of Masses on the schedule because the parish was losing an associate and the pastor would be the only one available to cover the Masses. This was already a difficult pill to swallow for the parish, but what exacerbated the situation was that the pastor insisted on announcing a new schedule that he alone came up with. I, along with the other staff member, argued for some kind of input from the parish so that folks had some sense of ownership of the Sunday schedule. He adamantly refused, saying, "I'm the one saying the Masses." The results were predictable: many people changed parishes because they felt shut out of the restructuring of the schedule.

"I'm the one saying the Masses." Pardon me, but I believe the rest of us have an important role as well!

Today's Catholics simply will not be as docile as they were decades ago, when they were taught to "pay, pray, and obey." They demand, and have a right, to be included in the decision-making process of the parish. Some argue, "The church is not a democracy." True enough. However, neither is it a dictatorship, nor is it an oligarchy. And yet, too often, the most that Catholics can hope for is that their parish be led by a benevolent dictator. Perhaps it made sense, in the Dark Ages, for the clergy to be responsible for most decision making, because they were far better educated than the laity. Today, however, a well-educated and more sophisticated laity will not sit back and remain passive when major decisions are being made that affect their faith life and spirituality. On the one hand, we can no longer tolerate a church that shuts out the laity when major decisions are being made. On the other hand, I don't think laypeople are asking for the right to elect their own bishops by acclamation, which often happened in the first centuries of the church (during the times of Ambrose of Milan or Augustine of Hippo, for instance). If we are going to be a church on the move, we have to engage in decision-making processes that invite participation and leave room for the most important person in the process: the Holy Spirit.

For a clue on how to do this, we can look to the example of the early church. In the Acts of the Apostles (1:12–26), when the apostles needed to appoint a replacement for Judas, they put forward two worthy candidates: Matthias and Joseph (called Barsabbas). Peter, however, did not make a pronouncement about whom he had chosen. Nor did he put it to a vote so that the majority would rule. Instead, they prayed first that God would reveal his choice to them. Then, they cast lots.

Huh?

Why would they leave such a major decision to a throw of the dice? Actually, they chose this method precisely to ensure that the decision was not influenced or coerced by any human will but rather reflected God's will. They left room for the Holy Spirit.

I'm not suggesting that every major decision in the parish be decided by a pair of dice! However, many parishes successfully employ a decision-making process based on consensus as a way of leaving room for the Holy Spirit. Engaging in consensus decision making is not necessary for every little decision that has to be made in the parish. But when a parish is faced with a major decision affecting the faith life and spirituality of the entire community, it is beneficial to engage in such a process with a representative group of people—most often, the parish pastoral council. Coming to a decision by way of discernment and consensus is about more than reaching a final decision; it is about forming a community of faith along the way. It stresses that how we decide is just as important as what we decide. So, what does consensus look like? Here are some general principles.

- The goal of consensus decision making is to engage in a non-confrontational approach to making a decision when there are deep emotions involved.
- The issue at hand is to be stated clearly, and everyone involved in the process must have an opportunity to state his or her views and to influence the decision.
- The facilitator (not the pastor) gathers the input and ideas of all the participants.
- The facilitator puts forward a proposal that incorporates everyone's input.
- Every participant offers his or her stance: support the proposal; temporarily pass in order to hear others' wisdom; offer amendments and changes; disapprove of the proposal with explanation and offer of alternative solution(s).

- Prayerful reflection and silence enable the group to ask that God's will be done and that the final decision(s) further the kingdom.
- Church teaching may need to be consulted to shed light on the situation at hand.
- Discussion continues until any areas of disagreement are reduced or eliminated.
- The process continues until consensus is reached, meaning that the final decision is one that everybody can abide by even if not fully in agreement.

Reaching a decision by consensus takes time and effort. It is, however, a Spirit-led process that enables participants to feel that they have truly contributed to a major decision in the life of the parish. In their book *What's Your Decision?* authors J. Michael Sparough, SJ, Jim Manney, and Tim Hipskind, SJ, remind us that a good decision is always preceded by a God decision. They remind us, as St. Ignatius taught, that God cares deeply about our decisions and that we can come to know God's will for us. This is true for individuals, and it is also true for communities of faith. If we are going to become a church on the move, we need to invite more people into the decision-making process and especially to leave room for the Holy Spirit.

*According to the knowledge, competence, and prestige which
[the laity] possess, they have the right and even at times the
duty to manifest to the sacred pastors their opinion on matters
which pertain to the good of the church and to make their
opinion known to the rest of the Christian faithful, without
prejudice to the integrity of faith and morals, with reverence
toward their pastors, and attentive to common advantage and
the dignity of persons.*
—*Code of Canon Law*, 212 §3

Questions for Reflection and Discussion

- When was a major decision reached at my parish without input from parishioners? What effect did that experience have on parishioners?

- When was I part of a decision-making process that involved reaching consensus? What are the advantages of such a process? What are the challenges?

- What decision is my parish facing now that would be well served by a consensus decision-making process?

- What major decision in my own life is going to require discernment? How does it help to know that God cares about my decision?

11

From Intolerance to Common Ground

Unity does not imply uniformity. It does not necessarily mean doing everything together or thinking in the same way. Nor does it signify a loss of identity. Unity in diversity is actually the opposite: it involves the joyful recognition and acceptance of the various gifts which the Holy Spirit gives to each one and the placing of these gifts at the service of all members of the Church.
—Pope Francis, meeting with members of the Catholic Fraternity of Charismatic Covenant Communities and Fellowship, October 31, 2014

If you were to take a peek at the playlist on my iPod, you would appreciate the fact that it is very "catholic." For example, you'll find the following: The Beatles; Johnny Cash; Adele; Daft Punk; Louis Armstrong; Simon & Garfunkel; Emerson, Lake & Palmer; Haddaway; Amy Winehouse; Gabby Pahinui; Buddy Guy; and Diana Krall, to name just a few. Rock 'n' roll, jazz, blues, folk, disco, pop, classic rock, Broadway, bluegrass—you name the genre, and it'll most likely be represented on my playlist. As I said, it's very "catholic"—with a small *c*, of course, meaning simply that it is universal.

We sometimes forget that we call the church we belong to "Catholic." Yes, the capital *C* indicates the denomination we belong to, but that word has a meaning: universal, all-embracing, broad or wide-ranging, comprehensive, and so on. You get the idea. And yet, there are many in the church who would like nothing better than to exclude others who do not think exactly as they do. If we are going to be a church on the move, we need to operate as a big tent and make room for lots of people who share the same core beliefs in Christ but have different ideas about how those beliefs are to be lived out and expressed. Protestantism, unfortunately, has not figured out how to do this. The result is an ongoing splintering that began with Martin Luther (although that was not his intention) and today is manifested in more than thirty thousand different Christian denominations.

Fortunately, the Catholic Church has found ways to accommodate differences. No doubt the best example of this is the wide variety of religious communities and movements that have found a home in the large tent we call the Catholic Church. Rather than moving apart into isolated tents, these communities and movements—Jesuits, Dominicans, Franciscans, Ursulines, Felicians, Carmelites, Benedictines, Claretians, Marianists, Norbertines, Passionists, Redemptorists, Paulists, Scalabrinians, the Community of Sant'Egidio, Focolare, L'Arche, and Regnum Christi (to name just a few)—have created a wonderful diversity within the unity of the church. Rather than allow splintering to occur, the church has found ways to embrace diversity.

St. Ignatius, the founder of the Jesuits, believed in profoundly revering each person as he or she is. That reality, however, is threatened today by those who wish to shape the Catholic Church according to their own narrow agenda. The late Cardinal Joseph Bernardin, former archbishop of Chicago, recognized this tendency and saw it as a dangerous threat to the future of the church. Shortly before his death in 1996, he founded the Catholic Common Ground Initiative in an effort to foster dialogue and lessen the polarities and divisions that threaten the unity of the church. The Catholic Common Ground Initiative continues to move forward, operating from the Bernardin Center for Theology and Ministry at the Catholic Theological Union of Chicago, working to "lessen polarities and divisions that weaken the communion of the church." (About the Catholic Common Ground Initiative—www.catholiccommonground.org)

In that same spirit, Pope Francis is renewing calls for greater dialogue within the church, calling for "welcoming those who do not think as we do, who do not have faith or who have lost it. And sometimes we are to blame. Welcoming the persecuted, the unemployed. Welcoming the different cultures, of which our earth is so richly blessed. Welcoming sinners" (Homily at Mass in Paraguay, July 12, 2015). Rather than attempt to create a homogenous community, parishes can celebrate diversity and seek to be cohesive, which is not the same as uniform. The key to doing this is not to try to placate everyone by offering various groups some occasional token recognition. Rather, parishes need to flaunt their diversity. Just as I keep people guessing about my tastes in music, parishes need to keep people guessing about which end of the spectrum—conservative or liberal—they can be pigeon-holed into, because those categories simply don't apply to discipleship. So what do I mean by flaunting diversity? Here are some examples.

- The parish bulletin and Web site can feature references to and recommendations for books that range from people such as George Weigel on one end of the spectrum to Joan Chittister on the other. In an attempt to practice what I preach in this book, I have quoted a wide variety of people at the end of each chapter, ranging from St. Josemaria Escriva (chapter 40), the founder of the typically conservative Opus Dei, to Sr. Thea Bowman (ch. 3), an African-American sister who was an activist for social justice, an educator, and a singer, dancer, storyteller, and evangelist.

- The parish can occasionally offer Masses that feature different styles of worship, such as a Latin Mass with Gregorian chant or a jazz Mass with a live band.
- The parish can "trade" choirs on a Sunday with a neighboring parish that features a very different style of praise.
- The parish can regularly sing the Agnus Dei (Latin for "Lamb of God") at Sunday Mass.
- Opportunities for enrichment and prayer should range from traditional practices such as novenas and the rosary to more contemporary practices such as centering prayer and reflection using the Enneagram.

Jesus said that "every teacher of the law who has become a disciple in the kingdom of heaven is like the owner of a house who brings out of his storeroom new treasures as well as old" (Matthew 13:52). A church on the move must not allow itself to get entrenched in any one "political" camp but rather must celebrate its diversity as a sign of the Holy Spirit.

We should not envision ourselves or any one part of the church a saving remnant. No group within the church should judge itself alone to be possessed of enlightenment or spurn the Catholic community, its leaders, or its institutions as unfaithful.
—*"Called to Be Catholic," Catholic Common Ground Initiative's Founding Statement*

Questions for Reflection and Discussion

- What factions exist in my parish community?
- What is the difference between unity and uniformity?
- What examples of diversity already exist in my parish community?
- How can my parish community "flaunt" its diversity even more?

12

From Business Meetings to Worshipful Work Sessions

The Christian is a man or a woman who knows to keep watch over his or her heart. . . . We need to test things—this is from the Lord, and this is not—in order to remain in the Lord.
—Pope Francis, homily, January 7, 2014

When I was in college, my dad asked if I would be willing to serve as the secretary of the Holy Name Society, the men's group in the parish. This took me a bit by surprise because I wasn't even a member of the Holy Name Society. When he told me that the position paid fifty dollars a year, I couldn't pass it up! So I became the recording secretary of the Holy Name Society at St. Casimir parish and the youngest member by about thirty-five years. Luckily, when my brothers and a few buddies found out that the meetings were followed by poker playing and free beer and sandwiches, they immediately joined, and I was no longer the only member under fifty-five. Within a year, my brothers, buddies, and I held the following positions: president, vice president, treasurer, recording secretary, and sergeant-at-arms. Our meetings were run perfectly according to Robert's Rules of Order: an agenda was followed, minutes were recorded and read, treasurer reports were made, motions were made and seconded, and majority-rule votes were taken.

Flash forward fifteen years, and I found myself in parish ministry as a pastoral associate, attending various parish meetings—staff, men's club, women's club, and so on—and most were following the same parliamentary procedures based on Robert's Rules of Order that I learned serving as recording secretary for the Holy Name Society years before. When it came time to form a parish pastoral council, however, I realized that Robert's Rules of Order left no room for the most important Person at any parish meeting: the Holy Spirit. Important decisions about directions for the parish were not to be reached by following parliamentary procedures. Instead, we forged ahead, relying on a format that can best be described as worshipful work.

The overall thrust of worshipful work is to transform any group, club, or leadership team into a spiritual community. Instead of following parliamentary procedures, worshipful work models itself after the gatherings of the early Christian community as described in the Acts of the Apostles, in which the Holy Spirit took center stage. Worshipful work sessions are characterized by the following:

- focus on the faith community's heritage and mission
- reading Scripture for guidance and inspiration
- theological reflection
- reaching decisions by discernment and consensus, not debate and majority-rule votes
- moments of silence
- singing and offering praise
- intercessory prayer
- spirituality over politics
- spiritual leadership over politics

- the people of God instead of a club, organization, or board
- formation of new members
- chronicling rather than recording minutes
- responding to God's call rather than taking roll call
- exchanging Christ's peace
- calling forth leaders rather than electing officers
- discerning of gifts rather than campaigning for office

Most important, in worshipful work, prayer is no longer relegated to the beginning and end of a meeting—the perfunctory bookend prayers. Rather, the entire session is permeated by a climate of prayer. The entire gathering is seen, not as a way to complete tasks, but as an opportunity to worship God and align ourselves to his will.

Much of my inspiration for worshipful work came from the late Sr. Mary Benet McKinney, OSB, and her seminal work, *Sharing Wisdom: A Process for Group Decision Making*, in which she emphasized that parliamentary procedures tend to favor those who are more assertive and vocal while discriminating against those who are more introspective. Even more significant, said McKinney, parliamentary procedure is a secular model and thus insufficient and even detrimental when used within a church setting.

So, what might a worshipful work session look like? Here's a sample outline (rather than an *agenda*) for a parish pastoral council meeting using a worshipful-work approach.

- **Call to prayer.** This can involve a hymn, invocation of the Holy Spirit, Scripture reading and reflection and discussion, and sharing of intercessions.
- **Response to God's call.** While a hymn is sung, those present are asked to prayerfully come forward and sign their names in a ledger as a way of indicating their presence and desire to do God's will.

- **Reading of the chronicle.** The chronicler for the last session reads his or her account of how the Holy Spirit guided the last session. The chronicle is then passed on to the next person responsible for chronicling the proceedings with an emphasis on the movement of the Holy Spirit.
- **Furthering the mission.** The "business" at hand is conducted. If major decisions need to be made, they are done through a process of discernment and consensus as discussed in chapter 10.
- **Thanksgiving.** The group gives thanks for the guidance of the Holy Spirit, either through a litany of thanksgiving or a hymn of thanksgiving.
- **Sign of peace.** Before leaving, members offer to one another a sign of Christ's peace.

A church on the move cannot be bogged down by politics or manipulated by people with political agendas capable of hijacking parliamentary procedures. Rather, a church on the move is guided solely by the Holy Spirit, and the only agenda is God's mission to bring about the kingdom.

––––––––––

When you come together, each of you has a hymn, or a word of instruction, a revelation, a tongue or an interpretation. Everything must be done so that the church may be built up.
—1 Corinthians 14:26

Questions for Reflection and Discussion

- Why are parliamentary procedures insufficient and even detrimental for decision making in a church model?
- What is meant by "worshipful work"? What can worshipful work accomplish that parliamentary procedures cannot?
- What experiences have I had of discernment when faced with making a decision?
- What experiences have I had with coming to a decision with a group using a consensus model? What are its advantages? What challenges come with decision making by consensus?
- How can meetings be an act of worship?

13

From Paternalism to Empowerment

*Do we support [the laity] and accompany them, overcoming the
temptation to manipulate them or infantilize them?*
—Pope Francis to Brazilian Bishops, July 27, 2013

While it's true that Jesus said we must become like little children to
enter the kingdom of God, there is no excuse for the church to treat
adults like children when it comes to their faith formation. And yet,
in too many parishes, adults who spend their days leading and managing small businesses, large companies, households, stores, teams,
and departments are made to feel like children when the church
invites them to a faith formation experience.

Just look at how most adult faith formation takes place. Folks
are invited to gatherings in which knowledge and information are
imparted to them by "experts," while those in attendance sit pas-
sively and try to absorb what they're being told. Now don't get me
wrong. The church absolutely needs trained professional pastoral
ministers. Today countless numbers of dedicated professionals serve
the Catholic Church as lay ecclesial ministers. In many ways, however, we have simply replaced one form of clericalism with a new
clericalism in which truth continues to be imparted in one direction—from pastoral staff members to the congregation—thus rendering the congregation passive. Pastoral ministers serving within

this paternalistic structure often lament how illiterate most Catholics are when it comes to their faith and assume, therefore, that no one can speak about their faith with authority unless they are in an official position with the church.

For years, few people were guiltier of this paternalistic approach than yours truly. Today, however, I refuse to do a parent meeting for sacramental preparation unless the parents can be seated in an area with tables and chairs so that they can engage one another in conversation. Likewise, I usually ask the catechetical leader ahead of time to invite four or five parents whose children recently received the sacraments to form a faith-sharing panel that I facilitate, guiding the panelists to share stories from their experience of walking with their children through that sacramental experience. Here are some of the questions I typically give a panel of mentors to reflect on as they prepare to share their stories about their child's first communion.

- What moment stands out for you as you look back on your child's preparation for and reception of first Eucharist?
- What does it mean for you to have your child regularly receiving the Eucharist with you on Sunday?
- How did you contribute to your child's preparation to receive the Eucharist?
- Why was it so important for you to bring your child to receive first Eucharist?
- What obstacles did you face along the way, and how did you deal with them?
- How do you respond to your child who expresses reluctance or asks why he or she has to go to Mass?

True, some of the panelists don't have all the vocabulary that comes with a professional degree in pastoral ministry or theology. But they most certainly are capable of sharing stories of faith and evangelizing one another. The role of the professional pastoral minister is to identify and equip people to share their stories and to stand by, ready to fill in the cracks with the language of church doctrine and teaching where needed. In other words, lay ecclesial ministers need to be about the task of equipping parishioners to act as mentors who, in turn, apprentice other parishioners into deeper discipleship. This concept of *apprenticeship* is one of the most exciting and challenging ideas that the *General Directory for Catechesis* brings us.

> This comprehensive formation includes more than instruction: it is an apprenticeship of the entire Christian life (67).

The whole idea, of course, is that those seeking to enter more fully into discipleship are to be mentored in the Christian way of life. Many pastoral ministers have been seeking ways to shape their ministerial efforts around this apprenticeship model. Unfortunately, we have been doing one aspect of this all wrong! Too many of us have been thinking of ourselves (pastoral staff) as the sole mentors and everybody else as the apprentices, when, in fact, our parishes are full of potential mentors we should be training and empowering to work with apprentices. This is the basis of our Catholic practice of providing sponsors for those preparing for initiation into the church; the mentoring is a shared task.

Today, experts tell us that over 70 percent of Fortune 500 companies offer mentoring programs to their employees. Rather than rely on a paternalistic system that centralizes all authority in the administrative team, a company mobilizes its existing employees and empowers them to act as mentors for new hires, apprenticing them into the life of the company. Such mentoring improves the health of the entire employee life cycle and improves new-hire retention rates while also developing the leadership capabilities of the mentors and grooming them for advancement.

This is precisely what we need in our Catholic parishes. If we are going to be a church on the move, we need to break out of our paternalistic mind-set and empower ordinary people to share faith with one another and to mentor others in the life of the church. Perhaps a good place to begin helping parishioners loosen their tongues would be at Sunday Mass, when we could invite them to voice aloud, during the General Intercessions, the names of those who are sick or who have died. Through such a simple act we can develop a parish-wide mind-set that the lay faithful are capable of articulating their faith in their own words and using their own voices. Are we truly empowering the laity to respond to God, or are we as a church attempting to respond for them like overprotective parents answering on behalf of their child?

Beware of speakers who tell you they must have an hour or longer because they cannot cover all that the participants need to know in a time shorter than that. This kind of attitude shows a lack of appreciation for the wisdom of the people.
—Jane Regan, "Toward Effective Adult Faith Formation"

Questions for Reflection and Discussion

- What experiences have I had of a paternalistic mind-set/ approach in my dealings with the church?
- In my daily living, either at work or at home, what responsibilities do I have that require me to act in a leadership role and/or exert authority? How could these skills be put to use in church settings?
- Who helped mentor me more deeply into the Christian way of life?
- Who have I mentored in the Christian way of life? Who might benefit from my mentoring?

14

From Parishioners to Partners in Mission

The lay faithful are protagonists in the work of evangelization and human promotion.
—Pope Francis, Conference on Mission of the Laity, March 9, 2014

One of the most sought-after achievements in the legal business is becoming a partner in a prestigious law firm. This achievement depends on the lawyer displaying a certain level of excellence. According to Eric Seeger, senior consultant with Altman Weil, Inc., once this level is achieved, the partner has certain expectations to live up to ("The 7 Habits of Highly Effective Partners"). He or she must

- generate income that covers his or her own salary (as a bare minimum)
- add value to the firm
- develop business for the firm beyond his or her own clients
- mentor associates and other less-experienced colleagues
- follow a code of conduct and be a team player
- contribute to the effective management of the organization
- represent the firm in the community.

The bottom line is, there are two sides to the coin of partnership: a partner enjoys the benefits of ownership in the firm while, in exchange, he or she contributes to the firm's growth.

Through the sacrament of baptism, we become partners with Jesus in his mission. We enjoy the benefits of the amazing grace that come with partnering with Jesus, not the least of which is our salvation! At the same time, this partnership requires that we contribute to the growth of the mission that Jesus has entrusted to the church. If we are going to become a church on the move, we need to pay more attention to the expectations that come with discipleship. And we can start by treating people who join our parishes as partners rather than as parishioners. By definition, a parishioner is someone who inhabits a parish. That's not very inspirational. For most Catholics, the process of becoming a parishioner is accomplished simply by filling out a registration card. Once your name is entered into the system, you receive your envelopes and, voilà, you're a parishioner. The problem is, when only a fraction of all those who were baptized regularly attends Mass, it is clear that the vast majority have little or no idea of the benefits to which they are entitled as a result of their baptism. And, of the small percentage who do attend regularly, an even smaller percentage do their share to further the mission of the church.

A church on the move must better articulate not only the benefits of entering discipleship but also the expectations that come with the reality of partnering with Christ. I recommend that parishes transition from the language (and the process) of "registering parishioners" and instead begin using language and developing a process for inviting people to become partners in mission. In addition to that, I recommend that parishes ask all existing registered parishioners to participate in this new process, which, at the very least, should include a small group interview/meeting during which folks are reminded of the benefits that are theirs when they embrace discipleship (the grace of Christ present to us in the Eucharist and in all the sacraments) as well as the expectations that come with discipleship (living as an authentic follower of Jesus Christ)—which are described below.

For too long, the expectations placed on lay Catholics could be summed up by using the age-old formula of "pay, pray, and obey." While some laugh about how this is the way things used to be, in reality, little has changed for the average Catholic who joins a parish. In researching this chapter, I did an Internet search of the phrase "expectations for parishioners." The first Web site that came up was from a Catholic parish that defined parishioner status as someone who "attends Sunday Mass regularly and uses the envelope system." I propose that we move away from the "pay, pray, and obey" definition, which is minimalist, and replace it with "grow, go, and bestow!"

- **Grow.** Partners in the mission of Christ enjoy the benefit of a relationship with the Lord and are expected to grow in faith, deepening that relationship through full, conscious, and active participation in Sunday worship and the sacraments, a life of prayer, and ongoing faith formation.

- **Go.** Partners in the mission of Christ enjoy the benefit of receiving the good news of God's mercy and are expected to go out to those in need, beginning in their own homes and extending to neighbors they have never met, to bring the good news of God's mercy to others in word and deed.

- **Bestow.** Partners in the mission of Christ enjoy the benefit of discovering their own gifts and are expected to bestow their gifts of time, talent, and treasure on the faith community and beyond.

In *Dedication and Leadership*, former-Communist-turned-Catholic Douglas Hyde asserts that one of the main reasons Communism was able to convert one-third of the world's population in the first half of the twentieth century was that it placed sizable demands on its members. He explains that Communism operated on the principle that if you require big sacrifices of people, they will respond. The theory was that engagement leads to belief, not the other way around. In *Growing an Engaged Church* (Gallup Press), Albert L. Winseman adapts Gallup's twelve rules of engagement and identifies how a parish can and must engage its members, beginning with this first rule: "As a member of my parish, I know what is expected of me." Engagement begins with clear expectations.

Jesus expected his disciples—those who walked with him during his ministry in Palestine and those of us who walk with him now—to be actively involved in God's work. A church on the move can articulate a simple vision of what it means to be a partner in mission using just three inspirational (rather than legalistic) words: *grow*, *go*, and *bestow*. Expectations that are articulated in legalistic terms will result in a minimalist approach, and, as Fr. James Mallon explains in *Divine Renovation*, minimalism has no place in the life of a disciple. Expectations articulated in inspirational and symbolic language such as *grow*, *go*, and *bestow* will elicit a heroic response, a response more befitting of a disciple of Christ.

The faithful, who by Baptism are incorporated into Christ and integrated into the People of God, are made sharers in their particular way in the priestly, prophetic, and kingly office of Christ, and have their own part to play in the mission of the whole Christian people in the Church and in the World.
—Catechism of the Catholic Church, 897

Questions for Reflection and Discussion

- Do I know what is expected of me as a parishioner?
- In the parish, are my spiritual needs met?
- At the parish, do I have the opportunity to do what I do best?
- In the past month or two, have I received recognition or praise from someone in the parish?
- Do the spiritual leaders in my parish seem to care about me?
- Is there someone in the parish who encourages my spiritual growth?
- As a member of my parish, am I invited to express my opinions, and are they given serious consideration?
- Does the mission/purpose of my parish make me feel that my participation is important?
- Are my fellow parishioners committed to spiritual growth?
- Do I have a close friend at the parish?
- In the past six months, has someone from the parish talked to me about my spiritual growth?
- In the past year, have I had opportunities at the parish to learn and grow?

15

From Presumptuous to Unassuming

At times we lose people because they don't understand what we are saying, because we have forgotten the language of simplicity and import an intellectualism foreign to our people.
—Pope Francis to Bishops in Brazil, World Youth Day, 2013

I never assume anyone knows who I am. From time to time I encounter someone I recall meeting previously some years before, and after I greet the person by name, I mention my name. In reply, I often get, "Oh, Joe, I know who you are!" In my mind, it would be presumptuous to think that I made an indelible impression on everyone I meet! My parents taught me to be unassuming.

Unfortunately, some of our Catholic parishes tend to be presumptuous. In my travels, I have the privilege of visiting many Catholic parishes, and I often like to imagine that I am a non-Catholic visiting for the first time. I have to say that in most cases, I don't find them overly inviting. On the whole, Catholic parishes are designed to cater to Catholics; we tend to presume that people setting foot onto our parish grounds are familiar with the layout, understand everything they see, know the vocabulary, and know what to do. Let's talk about each of these.

- **Getting around the parish "campus."** The McDonald's Corporation typically allocates about forty thousand dollars toward signage for each new location and erects a sign before ground is even broken. They assume nothing. Signs are a way of greeting and welcoming people, and they guide people to their destination. Many of our Catholic parishes consist of multiple buildings. Unfortunately, one of the things I often encounter when visiting a Catholic parish is simply the lack of signage telling visitors which building their meeting is in. I often spend fifteen to twenty minutes just trying to find the location of my presentation—and I'm the speaker! I find it particularly puzzling that a church that is sacramental—that uses signs in its worship—often fails to see the importance of signs for moving about the parish plant. It is presumptuous for us to think that everybody knows the way around our parish grounds! Realtors strategically place signs and balloons indicating the location of an open house. We should do no less to indicate the location of important parish gatherings to which we hope newcomers will attend.

- **Understanding Catholic vocabulary.** We Catholics like our vocabulary. In many ways, we speak a different language, and that's good. Unfortunately, we too often assume that everyone who sets foot on parish grounds understands Catholic-speak. And so we blithely announce that, for those interested in becoming catechumens, RCIA sessions will begin in the rectory; the Confirmandi should assemble in the sacristy for Kairos; the next CHRP retreat will begin after vespers on Sunday; and copies of the *Compendium of the Catechism of the Catholic Church* will be on sale in the narthex, with proceeds going to support the work of CRS and CCHD. I'm not suggesting that we not use our rich vocabulary. On the contrary, I believe that we can use it as a tool for evangelization. We must be constantly catechizing—that is, unpacking the meaning of what we say and do. In practical terms, this means that our use of Catholic vocabulary should be accompanied by a translation for those who may not be familiar with the terms we use. Otherwise we make them feel like outsiders who don't belong. Pope Francis said that we sometimes lose people because they don't understand what we're talking about!

- **Understanding what we see.** When people are in a room or building where significant or historical things happened, they often say, "If these walls could talk!" Luckily for us Catholics, our walls do talk! Ours is a sacramental faith, and we adorn our churches and buildings with many forms of sacred art. Once again, however, we tend to assume that everyone understands what they're looking at. Our walls do indeed speak, but many people don't understand what they're saying. Parishes should regularly take parishioners—especially new parishioners and adults and children in faith formation—on tours of the parish grounds to teach about the sacred images found there. Likewise, signage can serve to help people understand what they are seeing so that the messages of these sacred images can be received more easily by those who visit them. Such signage can play a significant role in evangelization, helping those who visit our parishes hear God's word being spoken to them sacramentally.

- **Knowing what we are supposed to do.** I once attended a parish meeting in which parishioners were invited to suggest ideas for enhancing adult catechesis. Thinking that perhaps folks would suggest Bible study groups or small faith-sharing groups, we were surprised when one regular parishioner—a cradle Catholic and a marketing professional—raised her hand and said, "I think it would be great if the priest could tell us what page the Nicene Creed is on!" As it turns out, since the new *Roman Missal* changes were put into place, most people in the assembly on any given Sunday still need a little help remembering the wording of the Nicene Creed. Many parishes provided pew cards for a short time to help parishioners get

more used to the *Roman Missal* changes, but those quickly dis-
appeared, and people were left on their own to navigate
through the Mass. Frankly, I think such pew cards should be a
permanent feature and should be mandatory for Masses with
children in parish religious-education programs and Catholic
schools. As a catechist, I have observed children attending
such Masses and not participating at all except for the Our
Father. We presume that since they are baptized and are participating in Catholic formation, they know the Mass. They
don't. And while worship missals can be helpful, most people
don't know how to navigate them.

We can help people engage with their faith and experience intimacy
with God simply by offering newcomers welcoming signage, a less
intimidating vocabulary, a deeper understanding of their new sacred
surroundings, and aids that help them participate more fully in
worship.

———————————

God does not suffer presumption in anyone but himself.
—attributed to Herodotus

Questions for Reflection and Discussion

- If someone were visiting my parish for the first time, what challenges/obstacle might he or she face?
- Where can my parish benefit from increased signage? What events in my parish could benefit from better signage?
- In a typical bulletin of my parish, what examples do I find of announcements that use vocabulary that is foreign to many people?
- What could be done in my parish to encourage greater participation in the Mass?

16

From "Turning the Page" to Meaningful Healing

Peace is something we must create piece by piece, with every
little gesture in our daily lives.
—Pope Francis, May 25, 2014

I have known and worked with hundreds of priests throughout my lifetime; most of them are good, holy men. Unfortunately, there are fifteen priests who stand out for the wrong reason: these are priests I've known personally who have been removed from ministry as a result of credible allegations of sexual misconduct. Among these fifteen are priests who served as my pastor, associate pastor, fellow faculty member, college professor, diocesan department head, and former student. Several of them are in jail. I trusted each of these men, and this trust was betrayed. I am not alone. Countless numbers of Catholics who were served by these men, were baptized by them or had children baptized by them or receive first communion from them, were married by them, and heard them preach about what it means to follow Jesus, were betrayed by them and by the church that failed to act properly when their crimes came to light.

When trust is broken, it takes time to heal. When people are betrayed in an intimate relationship, they often conclude that it will not be possible to trust again—and trust is key to any healthy relationship. Trust enables us to move forward. Broken trust, on the other hand, paralyzes us. The rebuilding of trust is a long and arduous process. For a relationship rocked by betrayal to be reconciled, true forgiveness is necessary. This is not about pointing fingers of blame, for all of us are a mix of saint and sinner. This is about reestablishing trust and moving forward together after a particularly egregious and widespread betrayal of trust.

Experts tell us that, while the capacity of a relationship to experience true reconciliation relies on the response of both parties, it relies especially heavily on the response of the betrayer. Much as builders in ancient Rome were required to be the first to stand under arches they built, one who has betrayed trust must show through his or her actions that he is truly sorry, is accountable, and can be trusted as both parties move forward. It is precisely for this reason that the church has long taught the necessity of performing penance as part of the process of reconciliation.

From the time that we are children, we are taught as Catholics that true reconciliation consists of contrition, confession, absolution, and satisfaction. Satisfaction refers to the act of doing penance. Penance is action performed to repair the damage and harm caused by one's sin in order to heal the relationship between oneself and one's neighbor, and also one's relationship with God. Such penance should correspond to the gravity of the sin. Penance equal to the sin has not taken place to help repair the profound damage caused by the actions of predators who sexually abused children and those in leadership who covered up their crimes, sometimes even by transferring them from parish to parish. As a result, we are living with a serious trust deficit in the church.

We must face up to this painful reality: we will not become a church on the move until this despicable chapter in our church's history is dealt with properly. True, the bishops apologized and issued a Charter for the Protection of Children and Young People at their meeting in Dallas in 2002. Likewise, it's true that reparations have been made to abuse victims through financial settlements adding up to literally billions of dollars. That reparation, however, is a civil matter. In one such settlement in a large diocese in 2015, the bishop presiding over the settlement announced it by saying, "Today, we turn the page on a terrible part of our history." The truth is, after trust has been betrayed, turning the page is not something that can be done that quickly. What has yet to be offered is spiritual reparations to the faithful in general—some outward sign from the bishops to the faithful that there is true remorse for the breach of trust that has occurred.

What might such penance look like?

The bishops might commit to working alongside other volunteers in a soup line, a homeless shelter, or a food pantry (or some other form of service to others) several times per month for a year as an act of reparation, inviting fellow priests and parishioners to join them so that the gesture of penance is seen as an expression of healing for all parties involved.

One might ask, what would this symbolic act really accomplish? Would healing really take place? Yes, in the same way that healing takes place when a parent offers to "kiss and make better" a child's scrape or cut. Few parents would state that they actually believe a cut or scrape will physically heal faster if they kiss it, yet most parents would not hesitate to offer that symbolic act because they know it will "make things better." Symbolic healing is real healing, and as a sacramental church, we should get that. If we are to be a church on the move, we need some healing. I know I need something to make it better. *We* need something to make it better.

The church, though battered and bruised, is the people of God. We are particularly battered and bruised and in need of healing. This is not a matter of wanting to see church leadership humbled or humiliated. It is a matter of addressing a very real and serious wound that continues to fester and cries out for healing. The bishops, in their role as our pastors, hold the key to that healing, a healing that requires much more than words. It requires symbolic action—penance—so that we can once again become a church on the move. After St. Peter denied our Lord, he did not try to put a spin on the story or bury it, but rather, he "wept bitterly." As of the writing of this book, a betrayed community of faith has seen no such act of penance from church leadership that might restore the trust that was so profoundly shattered.

The crisis, in truth, is about a profound loss of confidence by the faithful in our leadership as shepherds. . . . Only by truthful confession, heartfelt contrition and firm purpose of amendment can we hope to receive the generous mercy of God and the forgiveness of our brothers and sisters. The penance that is necessary here is not the obligation of the church at large in the United States, but the responsibility of the bishops ourselves.
—Bishop Wilton Gregory, then-president of USCCB,
June 14, 2002

Questions for Reflection and Discussion

- When did someone perform a symbolic action that brought healing to a situation?
- Does kissing a child's "ouchie" really make it better? Why or why not?
- Why is symbolic action needed on the part of the bishops to heal the wounds of the priest sex-abuse crisis?
- What penance would be appropriate for the bishops to perform to bring about healing of the harm caused by the priest sex-abuse scandal?

17

From the Stone Age to the Digital Age

A culture of encounter demands that we be ready not only to give, but also to receive. Media can help us greatly in this. . . . This is something truly good, a gift from God.
—Pope Francis, 48th World Communications Day, June 1, 2014

First impressions are very important. We all know that. Unfortunately we are not always aware of when and how that first impression is being made. Back in the day, first impressions were usually made face-to-face. With the dawning of the digital age, that is no longer always the case. In fact, in most cases, people's first impressions are shaped by online presence and social media. What this means when it comes to the life of our parishes is, that, for many people, the first point of contact with a parish is not its curb appeal, its majestic spires or rose window, the greeters, the receptionist, or the pastor, but rather its online presence. In fact, according to Grey Matter research, more than 17 million non-churchgoers visited a church Web site in a twelve-month period between 2011 and 2012 (*Christianity Today*, May 31, 2012).

So what are people finding when they visit the online presence of Catholic parishes? On the whole, Catholic parishes' online presence has improved, but in my own humble opinion, they still have a long way to go! When I search various parish Web sites, for example, I often encounter outdated information, cheesy background music, gaudy background colors and flashing images, a mishmash of fonts and font sizes, impossible navigation, overly pious imagery, churchy vocabulary and acronyms, and an unfortunate dearth of information that makes one wonder if the parish is still operating.

On the one hand, perhaps these shortcomings are understandable for a church that announces to the world that it has a new pope by blowing white smoke out of a chimney. On the other hand, if the majority of people are now making (or attempting to make) first contact with our parishes through our Web sites, we had better make sure the Web sites are up to snuff. If we are going to be a church on the move, we need to get out of the Stone Age and enter the digital age—pronto! Social media is not a fad. It is no longer a question of "Should we?" but rather "How will we?"

As always, there are real obstacles: lack of tech-savvy staff, little to no budget, and no time to maintain and monitor all kinds of parish social-media ventures. But even if all of the above are true, that's no excuse: there are people in your congregation (especially young people) who are capable of doing all these things with minimal financial investment from the parish budget. In fact, this is an opportunity for you to invite people with these talents—folks who may not be drawn to other, more "churchy" activities—to use their gifts in service to the parish.

The biggest challenge in developing an online presence is a lot like the challenge a family faces when getting a dog: care and feeding! Establishing an online presence does little good unless there are people designated to keep it current. I propose that every parish form a communications ministry to oversee establishing and maintaining an effective online presence that might include the following.

- Establish and maintain a well-designed parish Web site, keeping in mind the following best practices:
  - Know your "brand," your community, and the message you want to convey to them.
  - Include a "welcome" video from the pastor as well as brief testimonial videos from parishioners.
  - Keep it simple, clean, and easily navigable. As my friend Ray Ives likes to say, "Make sure it has good bones." In other words, be sure the site has a strong structure that highlights
    - location
    - core beliefs
    - service times
    - about us
    - leader profiles
    - ministries
    - what to expect upon visiting
    - what is expected of parishioners
    - upcoming events
    - contact info
  - Keep it current; retired and even homebound members of the parish who have online skills can form a "ministry of surfing" to ensure that info is up to date.
  - Plan ahead.
  - Make sure the site is mobile-friendly.
  - Set up an e-mail address to a person (who is named and pictured) whose job it will be to receive inquiries and respond promptly. Do this instead of supplying an impersonal contact form.
  - Include photo galleries.

- Make it possible for people to submit prayer requests—in a way that will maintain confidentiality.
- Consider offering printable, audio, and/or video recordings of weekly homilies.
- The pastor, deacon, or pastoral associate should consider hosting a blog (posting at least twice per week) to enable an ongoing conversation related to critical spiritual and pastoral issues.

• Set up a parish Facebook page as well as Twitter, Instagram, and Pinterest accounts. Whereas your Web page speaks primarily to existing parishioners, social media is designed to reach new people while also helping your existing community to coalesce.

• Have one or more persons in place who can effectively and pastorally respond to people via social media. Think of them as online catechists: they don't have to know everything, but they need to know how to respond and how to get back to people with the right info—something that, when done well and with care, builds trust.

• Regularly post on social media pictures of events, with brief descriptions and invitations to future events.

• Build an e-mail list so that you can more easily communicate with your existing community, and develop an e-newsletter that goes out monthly to keep parishioners up to date on parish events. Use this to share photos and stories.

• Arrange for someone to be on hand for all major parish events to take pictures of people in action, in prayer, and in service to others, and to immediately upload them to the parish social-media sites. Check "safe-church" policies regarding photographs that include children.

George Bernard Shaw purportedly said that "the single biggest problem in communication is the illusion that it has taken place." As a church we too often assume that our message has already been communicated, when, in reality, the message of Jesus must be proclaimed every minute of every day. St. Ignatius's concept of *magis*—always seeking "the more"—should inspire a parish's online efforts, driving us to do more to reach people with God's saving word. If we are going to be a church on the move, we need to utilize the technology at our fingertips to bring to the world the good news of Jesus Christ.

Communication leads to community, that is, to understanding,
intimacy and mutual valuing.
—attributed to Rollo May

Questions for Reflection and Discussion

- What Web site has made a favorable first impression on me? An unfavorable impression?
- Is my parish Web site welcoming? Is it easily navigable? Does it provide the most critical information? Does it tell stories and share pictures?
- What could make my parish Web site more effective?
- What forms of social media is my parish utilizing effectively? What forms could it utilize more effectively?

18

From "Please Help Us" to "Let's Build Something Together"

We priests tend to clericalize the laity. We don't realize it, but it is as if we infect them with our own thing. And the laity—not all, but many—ask us on their knees to clericalize them because it's more comfortable to be an altar server than the protagonist of a lay path.
—Pope Francis, interviewed when Cardinal Archbishop Bergoglio, November 9, 2011

Imagine parents throwing a party to show their appreciation to their children for doing their chores. At the dinner, Mom and Dad stand up and say, "We'd like to thank Frankie Jr. for taking out the garbage, and Elizabeth for doing such a marvelous job of washing the dishes. And, of course, we can't forget little Sammy, for all of the times that he takes our little dog, Buttons, out for a walk, even in the cold and rain. We couldn't do it without you!"

Sounds a bit silly, doesn't it? Children are taught to do their chores not as a way of helping their parents but as a way of coming to assume their own responsibilities. Certainly we can and should affirm our children for being good kids and for doing their chores regularly and properly. But to thank them for doing what is the minimum expectation—doing that which is their duty and responsibility—is to suggest that the chores really are the responsibility of the parents and that the kids are just pitching in to help.

Which brings us to the annual parish appreciation dinner. For some reason, we seem to feel the need to thank parishioners for doing what they have been called to do by virtue of their baptism. By thanking them, we are sending the wrong message: we are telling them that the parish staff has a lot of work to do and needs some assistance to get it done. I'm not suggesting that we do away with appreciation dinners—they can be important opportunities to affirm people for the great work they do in sharing their gifts with others. I do propose, however, that we change the name of the event. Instead of "appreciation dinner," I suggest that we call such events "A Celebration of Ministries," "A Celebration of Gifts," "A Celebration of Service," or some other name that makes it clear that what is being celebrated is not the thoughtful assistance that folks have given to the parish staff but the presence of the Holy Spirit in the community calling people to recognize and share their gifts with others.

Such a celebration of ministries should take on a prayerful climate, with the centerpiece being a renewal of baptismal promises and a celebration of the gifts of the Holy Spirit showered upon us through the sacrament of confirmation. I have worked at a Jesuit ministry (Loyola Press) for many years, and a phrase of St. Ignatius's that we hear and say often is "people for others." A parish celebration should reaffirm our call to be people for others.

If we are going to become a church on the move, we need to embrace, finally, the most radical message of the Second Vatican Council: the role of the laity and the universal call to holiness. Too often, the Second Vatican Council has been seen as a rallying cry for laity to become more involved in ecclesial roles that were previously reserved for clerics. While lay ecclesial ministry has indeed been a positive and significant development since the Second Vatican

Council, the Council has resulted in a new form of lay clericalism and has tended to overshadow the more significant call for the laity to go forth and transform the world. An annual event to celebrate the vocation of the laity and to affirm people who are indeed living out this call can become an important way for any parish to form people with an understanding of their baptismal call to holiness and to transforming the world.

When I was serving as a pastoral associate in a Chicago parish, I persuaded the pastor to rename the annual appreciation dinner "A Celebration of Ministries." Very little about the party actually changed: it took place at the same time of the year; the food was good, there was music and dancing, and everyone had a good time. Instead of the event being billed as a thank-you for helping, however, it was positioned as an affirmation of the many ways that laypeople were living out their baptismal call to holiness.

- Catechists were not simply thanked for helping make the DRE's life easier but were affirmed for sharing their faith with others and forming them as disciples of Christ.
- Ministers of care were not simply thanked for helping lessen the pastor's volume of "sick calls" but were affirmed for bringing the presence of Christ to those unable to come to church.
- Liturgical ministers were not simply thanked for assisting Father at Mass but were affirmed for using their gifts to help the entire assembly engage in meaningful worship.
- Parish pastoral council members were not simply thanked for helping Father make decisions but were affirmed for using their gifts to form the People of God in the local community.
- Members of the social ministry team were not simply thanked for helping the staff reach more people but were affirmed for making the church present to those in need.

. . . and so on.

If a church on the move were to utilize TV commercials to attract more people to ministry, those commercials would not look like those tear-jerker Sarah McLachlan ads for the American Society for the Prevention of Cruelty to Animals. Rather, they would look like the commercials for Lowe's that used to end with the tag line "Let's build something together." A church on the move must not simply be seeking assistance from a pool of generous parishioners but rather must be about the business of "building something together."

The laity [. . .] are called in a special way to make the church present and operative in those places and circumstances where only through them can it become the salt of the earth. Thus, every [lay person], in virtue of the very gifts bestowed . . ., is at the same time a witness and a living instrument of the mission of the Church itself "according to the measure of Christ's bestowal."
—Lumen Gentium, 33

Questions for Reflection and Discussion

- Does my parish have an annual appreciation celebration? What message do I think parishioners take away from this event?

- What does it mean to say that one result of the Second Vatican Council has been a new form of clericalism that can be referred to as lay clericalism?

- Why is it fair to say that the vocation of the laity and the universal call to holiness are more significant developments to come out of the Second Vatican Council than the changes in the Mass?

- How am I making the "church present and fruitful" to those I encounter in daily living?

19

From Clinging to the Past to Making Way for the Future

God is not afraid of new things.
—Pope Francis, Beatification of Pope Paul VI, October 19, 2014

In a humorous scene from my all-time favorite *Star Trek* movie, *The Wrath of Khan*, Admiral Kirk, now a paper pusher, comes aboard the *USS Enterprise* to inspect the training crew under Captain Spock's tutelage. As they prepare to leave space dock, Captain Spock decides to try something new and different: he asks a young trainee, Lt. Saavik (played by a young Kirstie Allie) if she has ever piloted a starship out of space dock, to which she replies, "Never, sir." Spock proceeds to hand over the captain's chair to her to pilot the ship, saying, "For everything there is a first time, Lieutenant. Don't you agree, Admiral?" The look on Admiral Kirk's face as he outwardly agrees betrays his true apprehension of allowing someone so young to take the reins of the ship he once expertly commanded. Doctor McCoy notices and asks him if he wants a tranquilizer!

Many times our church seems to operate more like Admiral Kirk than Captain Spock. While Spock was eager to give his young trainees some real experience, Kirk was hesitant and fearful of their youthful inexperience. It was only when an emergency situation developed and Kirk once again took over command of the ship that he placed his trust in the trainees and told them that although none of them expected this, he needed to ask them to grow up a little sooner than they had expected. If we are going to be a church on the move, we need to begin entrusting young adults with real responsibility and leadership roles, training them on the job, as Captain Spock did. If you need to take a tranquilizer, go ahead and do so, but we do our young adults a terrible disservice by making them sit on their hands while the same people are always asked to show leadership.

This is true at the national level and at the diocesan level, but most important for our purposes, at the parish level, which is where we will concentrate our attention. If only we look around us, we can see examples of young adults in the world who have risen to the occasion when given the reins of leadership.

- Jonathan Toews was voted the youngest captain in Chicago Blackhawks history (age twenty) and has since led the hockey team to three Stanley Cup championships in six years.
- Mark Zuckerberg launched Facebook when he was only nineteen years old and has transformed the way most of us communicate.
- Malala Yousafzai, a young Pakistani girl who survived being shot in the head by the Taliban for her advocacy of education for Pakistani girls, was nominated for the Nobel Peace Prize at the age of sixteen.
- At the age of fifteen, Savannah Britt began publishing her own magazine, *Girlpez*, earning her the title of youngest publisher in the world.
- By the time she was a twenty-year-old junior at Georgetown University, Catherine Cook created myYearbook.com and attracted more than twenty million members, earning more

than twenty million dollars in revenue, all from her dorm room.

- Although St. Ignatius was in his mid-forties when he gathered six companions in 1534 to form the Society of Jesus, the average age of his cofounders was twenty-four, with the youngest only nineteen!
- Jesus of Nazareth was a quarter of a century younger than today's average parish pastoral minister when he set forth to successfully proclaim the kingdom of God!

One of my favorite young pastoral leaders, diocesan catechetical director and blogger Jonathan F. Sullivan, once posted, "In some corners of the Church there is a consistent undertone directed towards young adults that we are there to learn or be learned about, rather than having anything meaningful to say on our own behalf" (March 31, 2015). We have to stop thinking of young adults as the "next" generation of church leaders and instead must begin placing them into positions as the new generation of leaders. I have made it a personal quest, over the past decade or so, to direct a great deal of time and energy to identifying and lifting up young talent in the church. For example, when Loyola Press asked me to write a book about the spirituality of the catechist, instead of writing it by myself, I sought out Julianne Stanz, one of the most talented young pastoral ministers in the church today, to coauthor the book with me. Soon thereafter, when I was asked to give a keynote address at the National Conference for Catechetical Leadership, an honor I had sought for many years, I was thrilled to share the spotlight with Julianne. I felt like Tony Bennett doing a duet with Lady Gaga, or Carlos Santana doing a duet with Michelle Branch! I was thrilled to be the "old geezer" associated with young talent that is on the rise.

So, what does this mean for our parishes? How can we begin to lift up and groom new leaders? Here are some suggestions.

- Be proactive in calling forth young adults to visible roles in liturgical and catechetical ministry as well as other leadership roles, such as parish pastoral council, communications team, and finance council.
- Identify workshops and seminars to which your parish can send young adults (the parish paying their fees and expenses), asking them to represent the parish, and then have them report through the parish bulletin, Web site, or social media accounts.
- Invite young adults to serve as leaders and facilitators of small faith groups.
- Invest in the formation of several young adults each year, calling them forth to participate in various formation programs offered by the diocese or other local institutions (such as lay-ministry formation or spiritual-director certification).
- Create a parish scholarship program to fund the formation of young adults in degree programs in theology or pastoral ministry, with the agreement that they, in return, serve the parish in some capacity.

In an article titled "7 Simple and Smart Reasons to Hire Millennials" (*On Careers*, June 20, 2013), public relations recruiter Lindsay Olson emphasizes that young adults are "eager to learn, are tech savvy and innovative, look at things in a different light, are adaptive, and are team players." Those are all qualities that a church on the move desperately needs and currently lacks.

Our answer is the world's hope; it is to rely on youth. The cruelties and obstacles of this swiftly changing planet will not yield to obsolete dogmas and outworn slogans. It cannot be moved by those who cling to a present which is already dying, who prefer the illusion of security to the excitement and danger which comes with even the most peaceful progress. This world demands the qualities of youth.
—Robert F. Kennedy, address at Day of Affirmation, University of Cape Town, June 6, 1966

Questions for Reflection and Discussion

- Who is a young adult I know of who shows great leadership qualities?
- What is the advantage of having young adults in positions of leadership?
- Who showed confidence in my abilities when I was a young adult?
- What are some of the ways I can personally contribute to the growing leadership skills of young adults?

20

From Slow-Moving and Rigid to Spontaneous and Flexible

In Christian life, even in the life of the church, there are old structures, passing structures: it is necessary to renew them!
—Pope Francis, homily, July 6, 2013

Every so often something comes along that garners the attention of a vast majority of folks in society who want to know how it "fits in" with their Catholic faith or what the church has to say about it. Think of books such as Dan Brown's *The Da Vinci Code*, Rhonda Byrnes' *The Secret*, or Tim LaHaye's *Left Behind* series, or movies such as Mel Gibson's *The Passion of the Christ* or, for that matter, any religious film that hits the big screen, such as Roma Downey and Mark Burnett's *Son of God*, Darren Aronofsky's *Noah* (starring Russell Crowe), Christopher Menaul's *Killing Jesus* (based on the book of the same name by Bill O'Reilly) or Ridley Scott's *Exodus* (starring Christian Bale as Moses).

What often happens when one of these books or movies becomes a phenomenon is that either the church issues a blanket condemnation (which results in folks lining up to read the book or see the movie in question) or the church says nothing and the secular culture catechizes on our behalf. This latter phenomenon is not limited to religious movies or books. Surveys show that nearly two-thirds of Americans base their understanding of the Kennedy assassination on Oliver Stone's movie *JFK*. If there is a vacuum to fill, Hollywood or the Internet will be happy to fill it.

This reality was the inspiration behind Bishop Robert Barron's epic *Catholicism* series. Bishop Barron asserts that the wrong people are telling our story and that the church is consistently being characterized in a very negative, narrow, and superficial way by these voices. He believes that we need to tell our own story. If we are going to be a church on the move, we have to be ready to move into action and speak to these phenomena and tell our own story. Unfortunately, we tend to have things on our parish calendars already that demand our attention and prohibit us from devoting the time and energy to issues that come along somewhat unexpectedly. As a result, other people—often the "wrong people"—end up telling our story and representing to society what they think the church is and what we believe.

Businesses face this reality all the time. They might find that all their energy and resources are tied up in doing things according to plan, rendering them unable to respond when a shift in people's tastes or new developments occur in the market. Unless they can respond with some degree of spontaneity and flexibility, someone else will come along with the appropriate response and attract their customers.

During World War II, the United States War Department contracted with Lockheed Aircraft Corporation and gave them just six months to come up with a prototype jet fighter that could fly at six hundred miles per hour; otherwise, the U.S. would face defeat. Lockheed, with all its systems and physical space wrapped up in designing current models, assembled a special team to oversee this project and gave them the autonomy to proceed unencumbered by typical bureaucracy and restraints. The team set up operations under a huge rented circus tent next to a plastics factory that produced foul odors; this is where they successfully developed a prototype for the P-80 Shooting Star—almost forty days ahead of schedule. Meanwhile, the foul odors from the plastics factory reminded one member of the special team of a story line in a famous comic strip of the day, *L'il Abner*, in which an old factory called "Skonk Works" produced such foul smells that people stayed as far away as possible. This suited the Lockheed special team just fine because they were operating under top secrecy. The team then referred to itself as "Skonk Works"—that is, until the publisher of *L'il Abner* objected, at which time Lockheed changed it to "Skunk Works." Today the business world still uses the term *skunk works* (along with terms such as *pirates* and *ninjas*) to refer to a team charged with quickly developing an innovative response to an unexpected challenge and doing so outside typical company bureaucracy and restraints.

I propose that every parish create its own version of Skunk Works—a team of pirates and ninjas—whose responsibility is to formulate quick and innovative responses to phenomena that pop up in secular culture and require a Catholic response. They would be, in some ways, a permanent "ad hoc" committee, not designed to oversee any ongoing programming but always available to gather when needed to respond to current issues. Here are a few principles such an ad hoc team would follow.

- It would be made up of parishioners whose leader would report directly to the pastor. (One of the principles of Skunk Works was that the manager needed to circumvent all bureaucracy and report directly to the top.)
- It would be free to meet off-site, preferably in someone's home.

- The number of participants would be kept small and manageable.
- The team itself would have no authority other than to present to the pastor a recommendation for how to respond.
- The pastor would then take the idea through the proper channels—staff and parish pastoral council—to get everyone on board and ready to move forward with implementation.

In most cases, rather than tell people not to read a certain book or see a certain movie, the parish can instead encourage people to do so and then come together to discuss and receive input that provides a thorough Catholic understanding of the issue at hand.

In response to the Protestant Reformation, St. Ignatius of Loyola felt it was necessary for the Catholic Church to tell its own story, and he recognized that traditional structures in the church were ill equipped to take on the task. His response was to form a more flexible and spontaneous religious community—the Jesuits—to get outside the walls of monasteries and speak to the world from within the world. It's unfortunate when Catholics get information from sources that are unreliable and erroneous simply because our parish structures are too rigid and formalized to allow for spontaneity and flexibility in responding to current issues. And it does little good for us to sit around and cry about how secularized society has become while we ourselves are not doing all we can to tell our own story. If we are going to be a church on the move, our parishes need to break free from rigidity and the tendency to move at a snail's pace and adapt the mind-set of "Skunk Works"—innovative responses with spontaneity and flexibility.

Spontaneity is a meticulously prepared art.
—attributed to Oscar Wilde

Questions for Reflection and Discussion

- What is an example from current events where the "wrong voices" are telling the story of the Catholic Church?
- What recent book or movie begs a Catholic response?
- When has my parish or another parish I know of provided such a response?
- When has the Catholic Church missed an opportunity to tell its own story?

Part Three

How a Church on the Move Worships

21

From Perfunctory to Robust

The Church evangelizes and is herself evangelized through the beauty of the liturgy, which is both a celebration of the task of evangelization and the source of her renewed self-giving.
—Pope Francis, *Evangelii Gaudium*, 24

When my brother-in-law Don, a Korean War veteran, was laid to rest a few years ago, he received full military honors complete with a twenty-one-gun salute, a bugler playing "Taps," and the careful and reverent thirteen-fold ceremony, in which the American flag was folded into a tri-cornered shape and presented to his widow. There was no skimping on the pageantry just because this soldier passed away sixty years after the conflict ended. As a result of this impressive expression of respect, the hearts of all present were moved.

When it comes to Catholic ritual and sacramental expression, the same should hold true: no skimping. Unfortunately, because of the multiplicity of sacramental celebrations, especially the Mass, we've grown lazy and have settled for perfunctory expressions of our rituals, all in the name of convenience. As a result, our worship—the most important thing we do as Christians—often lacks the richness and depth needed to inspire us to be a church on the move. So what is the answer? St. Ignatius believed that authentic spirituality is about awakening our deepest desires, which ultimately are from

God and for God. Our deepest desires cannot be awakened by words alone. All our senses—sight, smell, touch, taste, and hearing—must be engaged. Here are some general suggestions for taking a more robust approach to our celebration of the liturgy so as to engage all of our senses.

- **Smells (scent).** Our sense of smell, perhaps more than any of our other senses, is very closely tied with memory. We connect certain smells with certain places, events, and people. We also associate certain smells with church: namely, incense and candles. In addition to symbolizing our prayers rising to God and the cloud of mystery that surrounds God, the smell of incense calls us to transcend. While we may not use incense every Sunday, we can certainly use it more often than we do. If a few people with allergies or breathing problems limit the use of incense during Mass, assign someone to walk through the church with the censor between Masses so that the sacred aroma greets us without the smoke that may bother some people.

- **Bells (hearing).** Completing the second half of the classic description of Catholic worship—smells and bells—I'd like to offer a few words about the use of bells in worship. Bells call us to turn our attention to something important taking place. I suggest that parishes consider how bells can enhance processions. Bells can be used as part of a call to worship, and they can accompany the entrance, Gospel, and closing processions. In addition to bells, I highly encourage parishes to consider more variety of sounds to add to our praise of God when appropriate: drums, tambourine, cello, flute, violin, and so on. More about these sounds in chapter 24.

- **Spills (touch).** In the sacraments, we touch and are touched by water, oil, and hands. We need to use these elements more robustly, beginning with the use of water in sprinkling rites.

While it's appropriate for the Sprinkling Rite to be celebrated each Sunday during Eastertide, there's no reason we can't participate in a sprinkling rite at least once a month during Ordinary Time, using a more substantial aspergillum, similar to a branch or brush, that holds a fair amount of water so that the assembly actually gets wet. A few drops of water hardly comes close to symbolizing our drowning in sin and bursting forth from the baptismal waters to new life in Christ. Because our baptism is not a once-and-done event, it makes sense to renew it frequently and robustly. Likewise, it is not necessary for the priest to be the only person sprinkling the assembly. He can invite a corps of assembly members to come forward (a great opportunity to include young people) and to have each one take a section of the church to sprinkle.

- **Crumbs (taste).** Communion wafers are practical and cost-efficient; however, they do not resemble any kind of bread that we eat in daily life. When it comes to the Sacrament that is the source and summit of our lives, we should do away with practicality and use a more robust communion bread with ingredients that follow canon law (must be made of wheat flour and be unblemished) but that more closely resembles real bread. (Sample recipes for properly prepared communion breads can be found on various diocesan Web sites.) A ministry can be created in the parish, inviting families to take turns preparing communion bread for Sunday liturgies. Extraordinary Ministers of Holy Communion (lay faithful who are deputed to assist in distributing Holy Communion) can gather in the sacristy to reverently consume the surplus Eucharistic bread after Mass. Meanwhile, a smaller number of wafers can be kept in reserve for bringing Holy Communion to the sick and homebound.

- **Sights (vision).** Many elements of the Eucharistic celebration are intended to be seen. The décor and the various vestments, sacred objects, gestures, and movements of the liturgy are, in a sense, spectacles: something striking to view. One of the most important spectacles at Mass is the procession, an action that must be important since it occurs five times during the liturgy. I dedicate all of chapter 25 to processions and how we can make this a robust spectacle.

A routine is something we do in a habitual manner without thinking, such as the routine we follow each morning when we wake up to get ready for the day. Ritual, by contrast, is something we do in a habitual manner but with great thought and reverence. Too many of our most sacred Catholic rituals have become routine; we do them without thinking. It's time for us to think about how we can more robustly worship our God, whose love for us is never routine and is always robust.

———————————————

Every effort should be made to ensure that even as regards objects of lesser importance the canons of art be appropriately taken into account and that noble simplicity come together with elegance.
—General Instruction of the Roman Missal, 351

Questions for Reflection and Discussion

- On a scale of 1 to 10 (1 = perfunctory and 10 = robust), how would I rate my parish's worship? What factors or examples support my assessment?
- What can/should my parish be doing to make its worship more robust?
- Which of the suggestions offered in this chapter would have the most profound effect on worship in my parish? Which could most easily be implemented?
- Can I offer other suggestions for making worship at my parish more full of life and energy?

22

From Starting Up Cold to Warming Up

The liturgy is to really enter into the mystery of God, to allow ourselves to be brought to the mystery and to be in the mystery.
—Pope Francis, homily, February 10, 2014

Before any Chicago Blackhawks home hockey games at the United Center, fans are whipped into a frenzy, first by a video of the team's legacy accompanied by a dizzying display of pyrotechnics, then booming introductions of the starting lineups, and finally an electrifying and ear-splitting rendition of the national anthem accompanied throughout by wild cheers and applause. By the time the puck is dropped, Hawks fans are fully engaged and ready to participate, taking on their role as the "seventh man" in support of the six players on the ice.

Introductions at major events are important, because they help the audience transition and get ready for what is about to transpire. Major concert acts have warm-up acts, musicals have overtures, and TV shows filmed before a live audience often employ an audience coordinator to warm up the crowd by prepping them on when to applaud and generally getting them revved up. When the main act appears or the show begins, audience members enter the event fully engaged.

Why, then, do we assume that the assembly gathered to celebrate the Eucharist needs no such preparation? Most parishes I attend begin this way: the assembly straggles in and engages in small talk while choir directors/members and liturgical ministers dash about the sanctuary making final preparations. At the designated start time, a cantor or commentator says, "Good morning and welcome to [parish name]. Please join in our opening hymn [song title], number [number] in the missal. Please stand." The opening song begins immediately, the procession races down the aisle, and the assembly, many still filing in, is expected to lift minds and hearts to transcend this world and enter another realm, joining the angels and saints in their heavenly praise—a task rendered nearly impossible by the burdens, stresses, distractions, and tedium of everyday life. What we need is a little help making a transition. The introductory rites of the Mass are supposed to accomplish this. However, in our overstimulated world, we need an introductory rite to the introductory rite!

The liturgy is the primary vehicle by which we become a church on the move. However, the liturgy tends to pull into the station like a train or bus that doesn't quite slow down long enough for passengers to climb aboard properly. If we are going to become a church on the move, we need to do a much better job of preparing people to enter the liturgy so that the liturgy can do what it does: move people. I recommend the following as a more effective way of engaging the assembly and helping them become better predisposed to celebrate the liturgy fully.

- Five minutes before Mass begins, a commentator comes to the front of the sanctuary (not to a podium) wearing a wireless microphone or holding a microphone and carrying a clipboard or folder with notes, and greets the assembly enthusiastically, expecting and waiting for a response: "Good Morning!" [pause]

- "Welcome to [parish name]—a community of people broken by sin, but saved by the grace of Jesus Christ. For this great gift, we give praise to God!"

- The choir, music director, or cantor leads the assembly in a short refrain of praise, which, depending on its length, may be repeated. Instrumental music may continue in the background.

- The commentator proceeds: "Today, we celebrate the Lord Jesus on [day/feast of the liturgical calendar]. In today's Scripture readings, we [here, the homilist provides a two- to three-sentence overview of the theme that will be drawn from the day's Scripture readings and expounded on in the homily]."

- Once again the choir, music director, or cantor leads the assembly in singing a refrain, this time from the day's responsorial psalm. Again, this can be repeated, depending on its length. It is important not to introduce this as "practicing" the psalm response. One liturgical musician I worked with for many years insisted that singing is praying and we don't practice praying—we just pray (sing).

- After the refrain, the commentator continues: "Our community of faith seeks to put the gospel into action. To that end, here are this week's announcements" [unless the announcements are read after communion; see chapter 24 for more ideas on this].

- The commentator then concludes: "Please silence all cell phones and pagers. Let us take a moment to center ourselves and remember that we are in God's saving presence as we prepare to celebrate this liturgy." [fifteen to twenty seconds of silence]

- A short seasonal refrain is sung and repeated, followed by another five to ten seconds of silence.
- The opening hymn begins, and all stand as the procession enters; people do not need to be told to stand.

Spirituality is about our awareness of God's nearness. One of the key ways we deepen awareness is by listening more closely. We know that hearing is not the same as listening. Hearing is quite simply the passive act of receiving sounds; we can't close our ears as we can our eyes. Listening, on the other hand, is the process of actively receiving, retaining, deriving meaning from, and responding to sounds or messages. Our brains are bombarded with so many sounds that they must necessarily sort them lest we get over stimulated. As part of that sorting, our brains block out a great deal of sound; we simply ignore it. Like the characters in the famous *Peanuts* cartoons, we hear some people speaking, but to our brains, it sounds like a muted trombone: "Wah, wah, wah, wah." Any teacher knows that some specific strategies need to be employed to help students transition from passive hearing to active listening. Adults are no different. If we want to avoid having God's word come across to people sounding like "Wah, wah, wah, wah," we need to help folks transition into active listening at the start of Mass.

Listen . . . and attend . . . with the ear of your heart.
—St. Benedict of Nursia

Questions for Reflection and Discussion

- In recalling a major spectator event I attended recently, can I identify what was done to get the audience's attention leading up to the beginning of the event?
- On a scale of 1 to10 (10 being very distracted), how distracted am I when I arrive for Mass? What kinds of thoughts preoccupy me when the Mass is beginning?
- On a regular basis, how well can I recall the Scripture readings from Sunday Mass? The message of the homily?
- What would help me transition and be more ready to enter the Mass as a full participant?
- What can I do personally to shift to more active listening as Mass begins?

23

From a Wall of Sound to the Sounds of Silence

It would do us good to have a little silence.
—Pope Francis, homily, morning Mass at Casa Santa Marta,
December 12, 2013

I was not impressed with my experience of visiting the Sistine Chapel. I was most certainly impressed by Michelangelo's incredible masterpiece. However, despite calls of "Silencio!" every few minutes, the level of noise in the Sistine Chapel made it feel more like walking through a crowded gymnasium with a fancy ceiling than through a sacred chapel. Contrast that with the experience of walking through the Pearl Harbor Memorial in Honolulu or the Sixth Floor Museum in the former Book Depository in Dallas, where the silence is so profound, you can hear a pin drop.

Silence is a powerful reality, one that is underappreciated in our culture. That underappreciation for silence has crept into our worship and threatens our ability to move forward successfully as a church on the move. Noise has a way of numbing us. Silence, on the other hand, has the power to raise awareness—something that, according to the great teachers and mystics of the church, is key to a healthy spirituality.

If we're going to be a church on the move, we need to learn to be comfortable with the sounds of silence. In our frantic efforts to keep up with the megachurches, many of our liturgies have adopted an approach that can be characterized as a liturgical "wall of sound": a music production approach popularized by Phil Spector in the late 1960s and early 1970s that featured thick layers of overdubbed instrumentation to fill every possible space on the track. The result was that the layers of sound nearly drowned out the vocals. In liturgy, this "wall of sound" drowns out another voice: God's. In *Invitation to Love: The Way of Christian Contemplation*, Thomas Keating says, "Silence is God's first language." If this is indeed true, then through our lack of silence at Mass, we have effectively blocked out the one voice that can move hearts and minds like no other, God's voice that speaks to us in and through silence.

In *The Spirit of the Liturgy*, the former Joseph Cardinal Ratzinger (Pope Emeritus Benedict XVI), emphasized that silence should not be just a pause in the liturgy or an absence of speech but actually an integral part of the liturgy—a "silence with content"—the only appropriate response to a God of mystery who "summons us to silence." Silence increases our self-awareness, has a cleansing effect, heightens our other senses, and helps us solidify our intentions and motivation before taking action. Silence also has the strange and wonderful ability to unite people. Silence is dramatic and powerful; it amplifies the profundity of an experience. It is the most appropriate response to that which is beyond our ability to understand fully. In fact, author and Franciscan priest Richard Rohr, in *Silent Compassion: Finding God in Contemplation* asserts that silence is a necessary corrective for the spiritual life. He explains that without silence, we don't truly experience what we experience, thus eliminating its power to transform us. Experiences are important, but reflecting on them multiplies their impact. And silence is a crucial ingredient for enabling that to happen. I propose that every parish commit to integrating robust silence at the following parts of the Mass (as prescribed by the *General Instruction of the Roman Missal*).

- **Before the opening procession.** Even if parishioners are accustomed to greeting and chatting with one another upon arrival, there is no reason the assembly cannot be called to prayer and invited into a good two minutes of silence before being invited to sing the opening song.

- **Every time the priest says, "Let us pray."** Wouldn't it be nice if every time the priest said, "Let us pray," the assembly was actually given time to pray? I suggest about thirty seconds of silent prayer following every invitation to "Let us pray" to allow the assembly to pray in silence.

- **Following each Scripture reading.** To allow God's word to sink in, to echo in our hearts, and to call us to action, the lector, deacon, or priest should pause fifteen to twenty seconds at the end of each reading before saying, "The Word of the Lord" or "The Gospel of the Lord."

- **Before the Responsorial and the Gospel Acclamation.** Following the above pauses, another period of ten to fifteen seconds of silence would help the assembly recognize the profundity of what we have heard and are about to hear.

- **After the homily.** Anything worth listening to should also be worth reflecting on. If homilists knew that people would be given sixty to ninety seconds of silence to reflect following their homily, perhaps they would be motivated to give people something of deep substance to reflect on.

- **After each of the General Intercessions.** Although not mentioned in the *General Instruction of the Roman Missal*, I propose a five- to ten-second pause after each of the General Intercessions so that the assembly can really reflect on and pray for the petitions being offered. Specifically, when the assembly is invited to offer petitions in silence, it sure would be nice to have twenty seconds or so in which to do this.

- **After communion.** Receiving Jesus Christ in Holy Communion is the most profound moment of the celebration of the Eucharist. That experience should be followed by two or three minutes of silent reflection before we pray and are dismissed.

Evangelization is not about filling people's lives with more words and stuff. It's about helping people find and make space in their lives to encounter mystery. In order to do that, we need silence. Silence must not be thought of as inaction. Our Quaker brothers and sisters meet to worship in silence, practicing "expectant waiting" in which to actively hear God's voice. They take literally the advice of the psalmist who says, "Be still, and know that I am God!" (Psalm 46:10). If we are going to be a church on the move, we need to "be still" during worship so that we can hear God speaking to us and telling us where to go, why to go, and what to do.

———————————

We need to find God, and he cannot be found in noise and restlessness. God is the friend of silence. See how nature—trees, flowers, grass—grows in silence; see the stars, the moon and the sun, how they move in silence. . . . We need silence to be able to touch souls.
—attributed to Blessed Mother Teresa

Questions for Reflection and Discussion

- How well do I handle silence? Does it help me relax and focus, or does it make me edgy?
- Can I identify an experience that "summoned" me and others to silence?
- At what part of the Mass do/would I appreciate more intentional, robust silence?
- What does it mean to say that silence is not simply inaction or the absence of words and actions?

24

From Lullabies to Hymns of Triumph

Christian life is a battle, a very beautiful battle because when the Lord wins at every step of our life, he gives us a joy, a great happiness, that joy that the Lord has won in us.
—Pope Francis, morning Mass homily, October 30, 2014

For as long as there have been wars, armies have relied on music—marching songs, bugle calls, drum cadences—to fire up the troops or to strike fear into the enemy, or both. The "cadence calls" that continue to be used in today's military were brilliantly parodied in the movie *Stripes* when the characters played by Bill Murray and the late Harold Ramis led their platoon in a spirited singing of "Doo Wah Diddy Diddy" as they marched through boot camp. Rarely have I witnessed the same kind of robust singing at Sunday Mass! One exception was at a Veterans Day Mass in a Chicago parish in which personnel from all five branches of the military were honored. From the enthusiastic singing of "Off we go into the wild blue yonder" and "From the Halls of Montezuma" and "First to fight for the right and to build the Nation's might," it became obvious to me that battle hymns get people's juices flowing.

It's ironic, then, that on a typical Sunday, when we are to be sent forth from Mass to "fight the good fight," so many of our hymns have the unintended effect of lullabies. Some of these songs are sung in the first person, representing the voice of God comforting us, reassuring us, and pampering us as though we are frightened children, not unlike the lovely and tender song "Baby Mine" that Mrs. Jumbo sings to her little Dumbo in the classic Disney movie. Tender hymns have their place in the spiritual life, but if we are to become a church on the move, we need music and songs that will rouse the troops to go into battle. St. Ignatius sent forth his fellow Jesuits with the words "Go, set the world on fire!" Here are some suggestions for more effectively using music to fire up our "troops."

- **Singability.** Many of our hymns are either too complex or are sung in a key that is too high for most people, especially men. Anyone familiar with The Beatles knows that, for every album, John Lennon and Paul McCartney composed a song for drummer Ringo Starr that was within his limited baritone range, such as the incredibly singable "With a Little Help from My Friends," which ranges all of five notes. The fact is, most of us in the pews have vocal ranges similar to Ringo's, and yet most of the songs we are asked to sing have a vocal range better suited for John Lennon or Paul McCartney!

- **Song Familiarity.** Back in the day, when the National Hockey League had only six teams, it was easy to get to know the names of every player on every team. Now, with thirty NHL teams in North America, that's much more difficult. Similarly, our Catholic hymnals have exploded over the past few decades. While we have more hymns to choose from, the unintended result is that most Catholics are unfamiliar with a great majority of them. A good solution is for the parish music ministry to select hymns that will be sung for an entire liturgical season. With greater familiarity, the assembly can sing with much greater gusto.

- **Volume.** It's hard to sing when you can't hear yourself over the choir or cantor. After introducing a melody, cantors need to step back from the microphone for subsequent refrains and let the people sing! Likewise, instrumentalists can encourage better congregational singing by occasionally silencing the instruments and inviting the congregation to sing a refrain a cappella—suddenly the congregation hears its own voice and takes greater ownership of the song.

- **Drums.** A drum is a primal instrument with a sound that speaks to the core of the human person, resonating with our beating hearts. A slow and dramatic drumbeat can be used to signal the beginning of a procession: the opening, the Gospel procession, and the closing hymn in particular. Parishes have no shortage of teens participating in their schools' bands or drum and bugle corps who know their way around a drum.

- **Solo instrumentation.** One of the most moving pieces of music is related to the military: "Taps"—twenty-four simple notes played solo on trumpet or bugle. Most congregations have members (especially young people) who are gifted musicians: pianists, cellists, flutists, harpists, who can and should be invited on occasion or on a regular basis to provide an instrumental solo for reflection, perhaps after the homily, during the Presentation of Gifts, or after communion. This is a unique opportunity to invite teens and young adults to share their gifts with the church.

- **Chants**. In addition to standard hymns, chants (such as those from the Taizé community) provide a dramatic flavor to the music at Mass. Many chants also allow for drums. Some chants from Africa and Latin America are rousing and provide an opportunity for the assembly to sing in another tongue, thus expressing our catholicity.

- **African-American, African, Latino, and Caribbean music.** Whether or not a congregation has a presence of various ethnic groups, the music of these cultures is energetic, and it's almost impossible to listen to without being stirred to

movement. (African-American: "Soon and Very Soon";
African: "We Are Marching in the Light of God" ("Siya-
hamba"); Jamaican: "Alle, Alle, Alleluia!"; Latino: "Alabare")

- **Sung solos.** Few moments are more dramatic than when a
soloist sings "The Star-Spangled Banner" at a major event.
Although the music at Mass is not intended to be a perfor-
mance, there are appropriate moments for a solo voice.
Whether in a meditation song or a verse of a hymn, a solo
voice can add flair and even some drama to the musical
aspects of the Mass.

- **Energetic opening and closing hymns.** If any music during
the Mass is intended to get us moving, it is the opening and
closing hymns. These should get our spiritual (if not physical)
toes tapping and hands clapping!

The bottom line is, few things can get a crowd moving as music can.
We need to better utilize music at our celebrations of the Eucharist if
we are going to be a church on the move, calling and sending people
to set the world on fire, armed with joy and hope to fight the forces
of despair.

———————

*One cannot find anything more religious and more joyful in
sacred celebrations than a whole congregation expressing its
faith and devotion in song.*
—Second Vatican Ecumenical Council, *Instruction on
Music in the Liturgy*, 16

Questions for Reflection and Discussion

- What hymns get me moving? What are my favorite entrance hymns? Closing hymns?
- What is it about battle hymns and school fight songs that makes them so singable?
- After paying closer attention to hymns sung at Mass for a few weeks, which ones did I find unsingable? Unfamiliar? Was the choir/cantor too loud/overpowering?
- Has a particular musical experience at a Sunday liturgy roused me? What made this experience so robust? What elements of this experience could be standard on a weekly basis?

25

From Passivity to Processions

---

*I think this is truly the most wonderful experience we can have:
to belong to a people walking, journeying through history
together with our Lord who walks among us! We are not alone,
we do not walk alone. We are part of the one flock of Christ that
walks together.*
—Pope Francis, address to the Clergy in the Cathedral of San
Rufino in Assisi, Italy, October 4, 2013

Years ago, *Bozo's Circus* delighted Chicago-area children and their
parents; this daily TV show became one of the most successful
locally produced children's programs of all time. The show followed
a set pattern that included comedy sketches, cartoons, circus acts,
the popular Bozo Buckets Grand Prize Game, and, at the very end,
something called the Grand March, which was a parade led by
Bozo in which the entire audience gleefully marched, following Bozo
off-camera. While Bozo was basically leading folks to the parking lot
so they could return to their cars and go home, the Grand March
always left TV viewers with the impression that, although the TV
show was over, Bozo was leading the folks to some other venue
under the "big top" where the fun went on and on. We kids at home
even joined in by marching in circles around our living rooms or
kitchens so that we could feel like part of the movement!

Parades, like Bozo's Grand March, are symbolic marches. They don't necessarily lead to any specific location or destination, but they symbolize that there is a movement afoot. For Catholics, processions have always served this purpose. Processions are essentially holy parades, and Catholics have always loved a good procession. In fact, at Mass, when done correctly, there are five processions: we process at the start of Mass; we process at the Gospel; we process at the Presentation of Gifts; we process to communion; and we process at the end of Mass. We've also been known to have processions for May Crowning, Corpus Christi, Palm Sunday, and Forty Hours Devotion, to name just a few. At the University of St. Mary of the Lake in Mundelein, Illinois, where I studied for my Doctor of Ministry, in the conference room there is a photograph of an enormous procession that took place in 1926 at a Eucharistic Congress in Chicago—tens of thousands of Catholics marching first along Lake Michigan in downtown Chicago and then around the lake at Mundelein Seminary.

When people march together, it's a good indication that something is afoot.

We Catholics recognize that the procession is a metaphor for life. All of life is a procession—a pilgrimage or journey—in which we walk with one another, led by Christ, toward deeper union with God. We never walk alone. We never stay put. Someone is always leading us. It is no accident that the early church referred to itself as "The Way" (Acts 9:2), a name that expresses this movement and direction. To welcome people into the Catholic faith is to welcome them into the procession. With that in mind, to be a church on the move, we need to recapture, and effectively engage, Catholics in the art of walking in processions. This is not some form of nostalgia, a way to retrieve our glory days as a church when Catholic processions abounded. This is a strategy for engaging people in a movement and for reminding us always and everywhere that we are called to be a church on the move. I propose that processions become a standard practice in all aspects of parish life. Here are some suggestions for opportunities for processions (led by a cross and other symbols and accompanied by music and singing) in various parish settings.

- First and foremost, our processions at Mass need to be more robust. Too often our processions are paltry and brief. Processions need to be spectacles. The opening procession need not be confined to only one aisle; use all the aisles! Include banners, bell ringers, drummers, incense, and everyday parishioners to make the processions more substantial. Don't think of processions as the shortest distance between two points; go "out of your way." Gospel processions and offertory processions especially need to be "beefed up." And, most of all, slow them down so that they can be "entered into" by those observing them.

- Any time young people in Catholic schools or parish religious education are being "herded" from one of the parish buildings to the church for a liturgical experience (Mass, reconciliation, Way of the Cross, Living Rosary), that movement can be in the form of a procession.

- When catechists and Catholic-school teachers begin class, they can invite young people into a procession around the classroom, carrying signs and symbols (prayer cloth, Bible, cross, candle) to set up a prayer table.

- When parish meetings and gatherings (parish pastoral council meetings, parent sacrament meetings, organization meetings) take place, a group of participants/attendees can form a procession and carry signs and symbols (prayer cloth, Bible, cross, candle) to set up a prayer table.

- When people are elected or called forth to serve in leadership roles in various parish organizations, their installations can involve a procession in which the new leaders participate as a symbol of being led by Jesus (the cross) and of their own role in leading the group forward in contributing to the parish's mission. The procession can be accompanied by a Litany of the Saints; the group prays for their intercession.

- The social-concerns ministries in the parish can invite people to join in processions to raise awareness about particular social issues in the community, such as a procession through the streets of the community to raise awareness about gun violence.

- Parish sports teams can march in procession to their playing venue as an expression of their call to practice virtues in their athletic endeavors.

- Parish groups venturing forth on service trips, retreats, or local pilgrimages can gather in the parish for prayer and then be led in procession to the buses or other vehicles that will transport them.

Processions need not be elaborate, but neither should they be perfunctory. Bozo the Clown ended every show with the Grand March, a leg-kicking frenzy that created enough excitement to make kids at home join in. As a church on the move, we need to harness the less-frenzied but no-less-exciting power of processions to mobilize the faithful and send them forth into action.

The feeling remains that God is on the journey, too.
—attributed to Teresa of Avila

Questions for Reflection and Discussion

- How is a procession a type of holy parade? What is the purpose of a procession?
- What experience have I had of a procession that had an impact on me?
- What opportunities for processions exist in my parish community? Which of the ideas above would be most effective in my parish?
- If parades and processions suggest that there is "something afoot," what exactly is "afoot" when Catholics march?

26

From Pulpit Ramblings to Good-News Homilies

A preacher who does not prepare is not "spiritual"; he is dishonest and irresponsible with the gifts he has received.
—Pope Francis, *Evangelii Gaudium*, 145

For years, part of me has been tempted to publish a collection of the worst homilies I have ever heard. Sad to say, it would be one of the easier books to write and perhaps one of the longest. However, since I said earlier in this book that we need to do less grumbling, I will refrain from going on and on about poor homilies. But I do need to get this off my chest: for us lay folks, the reality of the poor homily is most frustrating because there is little we can do about it. It's not like we can volunteer to get on the preaching schedule. Is preaching every Sunday a challenge? Certainly. Any congregation can appreciate the fact that it is not possible to be spectacular week in and week out. There is no excuse, however, for poor homilies, which have no place in a church on the move. At the very least, worshippers deserve an honest effort. For a church on the move, Sunday worship is the most important thing we do. This means that preparing to deliver a substantive homily on Sunday must be one of the highest priorities on the schedule of anyone who is privileged to preach at Mass. As someone who does public speaking for a living, I can vouch for the absolute necessity of preparedness. So, with all that in mind, I'd like to humbly offer a few words of advice for homilists.

- Form a team of people (parishioners as well as fellow homilists) to meet with weekly to review the previous week's homily and to read, pray, and discuss the upcoming Sunday's Scripture readings and discuss what direction the homily might take.

- Be sure that your homily is an invitation to consider an alternate reality—the kingdom of God. The homily is not just a few tips for self-improvement, nor is it a refresher on doctrine. It is an invitation to consider a new way of living. In preparing your homily, ask yourself,

  ○ *What part of the Scripture readings proposes a new way of thinking, seeing, believing, and acting?*

  ○ *How can we practice this new way of thinking, seeing, believing, and acting in our daily lives?*

- This new way of thinking, seeing, believing, and acting—this Good News—is intended to replace some bad news. You need to ask yourself, *What is the bad news that my homily (and the Scripture readings) are capable of dispelling?* A good homily strategy is to begin with the bad news: an exposition of the problem(s) we are struggling with when we strive to do things our way instead of God's way. This, then, is followed by the Good News: an alternate way of thinking, seeing, believing, and acting that invites us into an alternate reality, the kingdom of God. Our world bombards us with stories that leave us empty, angry, confused, or in despair. The job of the homilist is to invite us into what author Brian Doyle (*The Thorny Grace of It*) calls "a better story."

- Summarize the "big idea" of your homily in one sentence. If you can't summarize the point of your own homily in one sentence, how can you ever expect the congregation to come away with a concise message? As part of their preparation, some homilists complete the following sentence: "As a result of my homily, the congregation will . . ." and they don't feel satisfied until that one sentence is compelling. Consider formulating the core idea as a question at the conclusion of your homily to invite your hearers to deeper reflection (and then sit in silence for a few minutes to allow that reflection to begin). You can then repeat that question just before the final blessing to send the assembly forth with minds and hearts engaged.

- Avoid scolding. Too many homilists introduce the "bad news" with an accusatory approach, pointing out what's wrong with certain segments of society. You need to point out what's wrong with all of us, including yourself.

- Don't settle for stories from a homily resource or from *Chicken Soup for the Soul*. Search your own life, and tell stories from the heart, especially stories that reveal your humanness and vulnerability. Be authentic, and make an emotional connection with the congregation. And don't consider stories to be fluff. Jesus taught primarily by using stories. One of the six reasons things go viral, according to Jonah Berger (*Contagious: Why Things Catch On*), is that the message is contained within the context of a story. The experts behind the very successful TED talks say that a good TED talk is about two-thirds storytelling. To learn about TED talks, visit www.ted.com.

- The other one-third of a good TED talk is gripping information or data, usually provided in no more than three "chunks." Follow up your story with no more than three points—three "chunks" of practical information that make the Good News accessible and replicable for daily living.

- Your homily is an invitation for people to embark on a journey. Start where folks are, here and now, and provide a solid reason for people to commit to the journey. Then offer insight on how to take the next step on this journey to transform the reality we live in.

- Invite the members of the congregation to post on social media one line from your homily that sums it up, captures its essence, is worth sharing, or struck them in any way.

- Finally, how you deliver a homily is as important as its content. Have yourself videotaped delivering a homily at least once per quarter, and view the video with your homily committee for feedback. Focus on your body language, facial expressions, and vocal variety. Do you come across as someone with whom folks feel compelled to walk the journey?

In *Divine Renovation* Fr. James Mallon explains that he models his homilies after TED talks. I can think of no better advice for homilists. TED talks are the most compelling examples of oratory skill available. According to the TED mission statement, the goal is to give people a new worldview: to "change attitudes, lives, and, ultimately, the world" by sharing great ideas. If we are to become a church on the move, homilies—whether they are eight minutes or eighteen minutes—must have as their goal nothing less than changing the world to reflect the values of God's kingdom.

People have an idea that the preacher is an actor on a stage and they are the critics, blaming or praising him. What they don't know is that they are the actors on the stage; he (the preacher) is merely the prompter standing in the wings, reminding them of their lost lines.
—attributed to Søren Kierkegaard

Questions for Reflection and Discussion

- What are examples of the best and worst homilies I have experienced? What made them either excellent or poor?
- What do I expect from a homily?
- What makes a homily effective?
- What one piece of advice would I most like to give homilists to help them become more effective?

27

From a Collection to an Offering

Life is not given to us to be jealously guarded for ourselves, but is given to us so that we may give it in turn.
—Pope Francis, April 24, 2013

There is no shortage of jokes about the Sunday collection. Here's one of my favorites: A little girl becomes restless as the pastor's homily drags on and on. Finally she leans over to her mother and whispers, "Mommy, if we give him the money now, will he let us go?"

It's easy to make jokes about the Sunday collection because we don't feel that there's anything sacred about it: it's just the way a parish pays its bills. That's unfortunate because this is not the "business" portion of our gathering at Sunday Mass. It is part of the act of celebrating Eucharist. It is a ritual expression of our stewardship, a sacred moment in which we bring ourselves and our gifts to the altar to be transformed and shared with the larger community. In reality, this moment of the Mass amounts to a huge missed opportunity. Rather than seize this moment to mobilize an army to change the world through a profound act of generosity, we reduce it to a convenient and painless way to keep the lights turned on.

I mentioned in chapter 21 that, for convenience's sake, we have gotten lazy in many of our liturgical expressions. The Sunday collection is the perfect example. Somewhere along the way, we decided that it would be easier, quicker, and more efficient if we had ushers go around with baskets to collect people's offerings instead of making folks get up and bring their offerings to the altar. And yes, it is easier, quicker, and more efficient to collect using ushers with baskets. The problem is, this is not a collection; it is an offering. The *General Instruction of the Roman Missal* tells us that after the altar is prepared, "the offerings are then brought forward" (73). It does not say that "the collection is taken up." And yet, for some reason, we have settled for the easiest way to get this done, forgetting that ritual is not about efficiency. As a result, this has altered the very expression taking place. We are no longer performing an act of offering; we are simply paying the bills. The focus is completely on what ends up in the basket instead of on the act of giving itself.

A church on the move needs a greater sense of stewardship. This could be instilled in the assembly if the offering/presentation of gifts were more robust. Instead of simply having ushers proceed through the church with baskets, the following can be done.

- A number of baskets could be set up strategically throughout the church before the Mass.
- As the song at the Presentation of Gifts is sung, the ushers invite people to leave their seats and proceed to the nearest collection basket, where they drop their offering. The act of leaving one's seat to offer a gift creates a greater sense of active participation in the liturgy.
- In addition, tables or baskets could be set up ahead of time in various locations in the church for canned goods and/or clothing for those in need. Parishioners can be encouraged to bring these types of donations in addition to, or instead of, a monetary donation. This will become increasingly important as parishes move toward electronic giving, which results in more and more people having nothing to offer physically on

Sunday. In such cases, people can bring in canned goods or clothing in addition to their electronic donation to the parish.

- Entire families can be invited to come forward together to present their offering(s) instead of one person dropping an envelope in a collection basket.
- The elderly and disabled can be invited to simply raise their hands so that ushers or fellow parishioners can retrieve their offering and bring it forward.
- When all have returned to their places, the ushers gather the monetary offerings into one large basket.
- Altar servers carrying the cross and candles then proceed to the gift table to lead those members of the assembly who have been chosen to bring forward the gifts, along with the ushers, who bring forward the monetary collection.

People give for many different reasons:

- People tend to give to charity when they are asked and when they believe in the cause. In a sense, in simply having ushers walk around with collection baskets, we are not asking people to do anything. To invite people to get up out of their seats to contribute their offering is to ask them to participate in a communal gesture toward a cause.
- People like to give because it helps them overcome a sense of powerlessness. Inviting people to "march" forward as one body strengthens a feeling of empowerment.
- People give when they feel a sense of closeness to a community. The collection basket reduces the offertory to an isolated act. To come forward in unison creates a greater sense of community and inspires people to give more.
- Finally, while this may not be the noblest reason, people give because they want to look good. An offertory procession

provides parishioners an opportunity to publicly show that they belong to a community of generous hearts.

As my friend Fr. David Loftus points out, bread and wine do not exist naturally in the world; they require our work. Something of our very selves is required before the "stuff" of our offering is possible. Too many of us Catholics take a minimalist approach when it comes to monetary giving (studies consistently show that Catholics on the average give less than our Protestant brothers and sisters). It doesn't help that, at Mass, we take a minimalist approach to gathering peoples' offerings. It should take work. If we want to mobilize people to be more generous with their time, talent, and treasure, we should literally get them up out of their seats and in motion. The Sunday offering is a good place for this to happen.

What do Christians bring to the Eucharistic celebration and join there with Jesus' offering? Their lives as Christian disciples; their personal vocations and the stewardship they have exercised regarding them; their individual contributions to the great work of restoring all things in Christ. Disciples give thanks to God for gifts received and strive to share them with others.
—"Stewardship: A Disciple's Response"—A Pastoral Letter on Stewardship, USCCB

Questions for Reflection and Discussion

- In what way(s) is the Sunday collection a sacred moment? Do I ever think of it as such? Why or why not?
- How is the offertory handled in my parish? What can be done to make this moment a deeper and more active expression of stewardship?
- What do I think of leaving my seat to bring my offering "to the altar"?
- What are the main reasons that I give to charity?

28

From Prohibition to Drinking from the Cup

*Since Christ's entire existence had a missionary character, so too,
all those who follow him closely must possess this
missionary quality.*
—Pope Francis, message for World Mission Day, 2015

Think of a hobby you enjoy: fishing, gardening, walking, or playing a musical instrument. Whatever it is, it does something to you, doesn't it? Maybe it relaxes you, inspires you, lifts your heart, lightens your spirit, or touches your soul. But the experience doesn't stop there, and the flow of energy is not all moving in one direction. This hobby also gives you an opportunity to express yourself. You can express your freedom, your desire, your passion, your creativity, your imagination, and so on. Experiences are both formative and expressive.

The same is true of our worship experiences as Catholics. The sacraments are both formative and expressive. On the one hand, the sacraments are not so much about what we are doing but primarily about what God is doing in our lives. The sacraments are formative. On the other hand, our celebration of the sacraments also gives us an opportunity to express ourselves and, of course, the Eucharist is our most profound sacramental moment. This sacrament, like all the sacraments, forms us. To paraphrase the words of St. Augustine, we become what we eat; we are formed into the Body of Christ. Receiving the Body and Blood of Jesus does something to us, but it is also an opportunity for us to express something about who we are in relation to God and to one another.

To "break bread" with someone—to share a meal—is to share a bond with them. In this way we enter relationship with them. This is why when we want to express affection for others, we invite them to share a meal with us. What we eat at such a meal is not as significant as the fact that we are eating it together. In the same way, when we come forward to receive the Body of Christ, we are expressing our communion not only with Jesus Christ but also with one another. I think that this notion is fairly well understood by most Catholics. What it means to drink from the cup is another story.

Even though the practice of drinking from the cup has ancient roots, it was only in the wake of the Second Vatican Council in the 1960s that Catholics were once again welcome to receive from the cup. Unfortunately, in many places the practice has not caught on, was never introduced, or was dropped. This is unfortunate for a church that wishes to be a church on the move. Why? Because drinking from the cup expresses our commitment to the mission of the church. When two of the disciples ask Jesus if they can be seated at his side in the eternal kingdom, Jesus responds by asking them if they are willing to drink from the same cup that he is going to drink from (Mark 10:38). Later, and more poignantly, when Jesus is suffering his agony in the garden—as he struggles with his own commitment—he asks the Father, "My Father, if it is possible, may this cup be taken from me." (Matthew 26:39). Jesus is tempted to abandon his mission. Yet he finds the strength to drink from that very cup. It is this cup that he now offers to us as an opportunity to express our commitment to his mission.

Receiving from the cup is not just a way of "getting more Jesus." In our reception of the Body of Christ, we have received the very essence of Jesus Christ—body, soul, and divinity. To drink his precious Blood from the cup is not to somehow get a double dose. It is, however, a fuller expression of Jesus' offering himself to us, and it is also a fuller expression of our commitment to Jesus' mission, the mission of the church, which we share by virtue of our baptism.

If we desire to be a church on the move, we need to encourage and invite the entire assembly, as much as possible, to receive from the cup and to understand why. To do so, we need to address people's hesitations.

- "It is unnatural to share a drinking cup." We usually share a drinking cup with those with whom we have an intimate relationship: spouse, children, sibling, or in some cases a close friend. That is precisely why this is such a powerful expression of our commitment: it is an expression of a willingness to take a risk.

- "It's not hygienic." One of the reasons we don't share drinking cups is because we don't want to pass or catch germs. This, again, is why the expression is so powerful: it expresses a willingness to face risks. Of course, if you are carrying germs or if there is a "bug" going around, it makes sense to refrain from sharing in the cup. Beyond that, there is actually more risk for passing germs by handling previously used worship aids or exchanging a handshake of peace than there is from drinking from a cup that is wiped after each sip and has alcohol content that reduces risk.

- "It diminishes the role of the priest." Some wrongly think that the proliferation of extraordinary ministers of Holy Communion (lay faithful who are deputed to assist in distributing

Holy Communion) to offer the cup somehow diminishes the role of the priest. This is nonsense. They are called "extraordinary" for a reason.

The truth is, it requires a lot of effort to recruit, train, form, and schedule an adequate number of ministers of the cup and to estimate how much wine to use so that there is not an excess of the Lord's precious blood that needs to be consumed after Mass. It is simply easier not to bother with all this "fuss." The unfortunate consequence of a lazy response to these challenges is, once again, a less robust approach to worship, which coincides with a more tepid commitment to mission and, thus, a church that is not on the move.

Forming, educating, and inviting people to regularly drink from the cup at Mass is a perfect example of one of the ways Catholic parishes can create a church on the move simply by embracing our own Catholic practices and doing them more intentionally so as to inspire people to go forth and set the world on fire.

Holy Communion has a fuller form as a sign when it is distributed under both kinds.
—*General Instruction of the Roman Missal, 281*

Questions for Reflection and Discussion

- What is the most important commitment in my life? When is it difficult to "drink from this cup"?
- How is receiving the Body and Blood of Christ both formative and expressive?
- What is my experience of receiving the Blood of Jesus from the cup at communion? What hesitations do I have about receiving from the cup?
- What in this chapter do I consider the most compelling reason for receiving from the cup?

29

From Announcements to Altar Calls

So let us ask ourselves this evening, in adoring Christ who is really present in the Eucharist: do I let myself be transformed by him? Do I let the Lord who gives himself to me, guide me to going out ever more from my little enclosure, in order to give, to share, to love him and others?
—Pope Francis, Corpus Christi homily, May 30, 2013

At most Catholic churches, after communion there are a few bland announcements about a meeting of the Men's Club on Tuesday night, a second collection being taken next week, and the Women's Club daffodil sale taking place today in the foyer after all the Masses. Not so at one Chicago parish, where the pastor effectively uses the time after communion to "mobilize the troops." On one particular Sunday that I attended this predominantly African-American parish, the pastor got up after communion and announced that he would be leading a group of parishioners to march that Friday evening on a nearby busy street to peacefully confront drug dealers, pray with them, and ask them to stop their activity. He then asked for volunteers to march with him. Little by little, a smattering of people left their seats and came forward to the altar to join the pastor. Before long, he was surrounded by an army of parishioners. He prayed over them and commissioned them to join him in these efforts. Sure enough, that Friday evening, local TV news outlets carried stories about an army of people from this parish, led by their pastor, marching through the streets of the community to confront drug dealers. As a result of this and similar efforts over weeks, months, and years, drug traffic and crime significantly dropped in the area.

What happened at this parish on that Sunday (and on most Sundays) was the Catholic version of an altar call. In evangelical Protestant circles, an altar call is a common practice whereby those who wish to make a personal but public commitment to Christ are invited to come forward following the sermon to be "prayed over." For Catholics, going to Holy Communion is our altar call. It is through the action of receiving the Body and Blood of Jesus that we express our commitment to Christ. What took place after communion at this Chicago parish was not an invitation for people to come forward to make a commitment to Christ. That had already happened in Holy Communion. What the pastor did was simply an extraordinary version of the "announcements"—on steroids. Each week the pastor announces how the church is going to heroically practice its mission that particular week and how folks can participate. It is a weekly "ministry fair" taking place within the context of the Eucharistic celebration.

Unfortunately, in most Catholic parishes, many of our ministries are well-kept secrets. At the heart of this problem is the fact that so many of our ministries are rarely visible as part of the liturgy itself. In most parishes, on any given Sunday, an army of people are present in the assembly at Mass, people who will be going forth to minister to the needs of others—heroically, yet under the radar. I propose that, after communion, we transform the reading of announcements into an "altar call" to highlight these efforts. It might look, sound, and feel something like this:

Pastor/Presider:

This week, our parish will be sending forth a number of people to perform works of mercy, both physical and spiritual, bringing hope to those in need.

This week, members of our St. Vincent de Paul Society will be staffing soup kitchens, PADS shelters, and food pantries at four different locations. If you are involved in these efforts or would like to be, please come forward. [Music begins to play in the background; people come forward to stand before the altar.]

Our religious education program has classes on Tuesday evening. If you are involved as a catechist or an aide or would like to participate in this ministry, please come forward.

Next Saturday, our youth group will be hosting a car wash to raise money for the homeless shelter. If you are involved in this effort or would like to be, please come forward.

As always, a number of people in our parish will be visiting the sick and bringing Holy Communion to the homebound. If you are a Minister of Care or would like to be involved in this ministry, please come forward.

[Once all are in place, the pastor/presider speaks a few words of encouragement and affirmation and then commissions them to go forth. He invites those who came forward to express interest in these ministries and activities to meet in the foyer after Mass for more information. The assembly then sings a refrain as all are sent back to their places and the assembly stands for the final blessing.]

Such an approach highlights these parish ministries, makes them more visible, grounds them in the liturgy, ties them to the dismissal rite, and invites people to join and support these ministries in an ongoing way instead of waiting for ministries to decay and then desperately seeking people to take them over. We come to Mass not simply for our own spiritual benefit but to be moved into action to serve others (remember our Ignatian term "people for others"?). Most important, this communicates in an ongoing fashion that this parish is indeed a "church on the move" and that the Eucharist is a call to repent in concrete ways and to take action to bring the kingdom of God to those most in need of experiencing God's nearness.

A Eucharist which does not pass over into the concrete practice of love is intrinsically fragmented.
—Pope Benedict XVI, Deus Caritas Est, no. 14

Questions for Reflection and Discussion

- As I listen to my parish's after-communion announcements, can I identify what types of activities are getting the most attention and which are being kept "secret"?
- If my parish performed an "altar call"—calling forth and inviting people to serve others in the coming week—what are some examples of ministries already in existence that would be highlighted? What ministries might my parish consider adding?
- What needs in my community are presently not being addressed, and how can my parish respond?
- How am I personally putting my faith into action, making sure that my celebration of the Eucharist translates into the concrete practice of love?

30

From Perfunctory Prayer to Worship Experiences

---

*I think—I say this humbly—that we Christians may have
somewhat lost the sense of worship, and we think: let's go to the
Temple, let's come together as brothers and sisters—that's good,
it's great!—but the centre is where God is. And we worship God.*
—Pope Francis, morning Mass at Casa Santa Marta,
November 22, 2013

If something is good for you, like physical exercise, eating healthy
foods, or getting enough rest, it makes sense to try to engage in that
activity regularly to enjoy its benefits. Scripture tells us that worship
is good for us. Worship awakens us, recalibrates us, clears the spiritual fog that settles over us, gives us assurance, helps us grow in holiness, increases our sense of joy, empowers us to do wonderful things,
humbles us, and connects us with the very source of our being so
that we know we are not alone.

God doesn't need our worship; we do. To worship simply means
that we direct all our attention to someone or something. We can
worship money, power, possessions, celebrities, or status, meaning
that we direct all our attention and energy toward them. What these
things give back to us in return is fleeting. When we direct all our
attention and energy toward God—when we worship God—what

we get in return is a sustaining relationship with the Creator of the universe.

No doubt this is why worship of God alone is the first commandment and also serves as the First Principle and Foundation of the Spiritual Exercises of St. Ignatius of Loyola. If we get that right, everything else falls into place. It's unfortunate, then, that we tend to limit our worship to once a week (if that often). If we are going to become a church on the move, we need to worship more often than on Sunday. And no, I'm not suggesting that every Catholic needs to attend daily Mass. I am, however, suggesting that Catholics find other ways of worshipping in addition to the Mass. Whenever Catholics gather, such as at any parish meeting, we have an opportunity to worship God. Instead, we tend to settle for a perfunctory prayer or the reading of an inspirational poem.

True worship is an effort to realign our minds, hearts, and wills with God's. It is an attempt to direct all our attention and energy to God rather than give a perfunctory nod to the existence of some nebulous force of goodness. A worship experience should take its cues from the Mass and should resemble elements of the Mass. I propose that every parish train at least a half dozen people to lead liturgical prayer—worship that follows a simple set order, with designated roles such as *leader, reader,* and *all.* I also propose that every parish assemble at least a half dozen worship kits to provide prayer leaders with some tools that greatly enhance worshipful prayer.

Let's start with worship kits. I created several of these at Loyola Press for our educational consultants to use if they are called upon to lead prayer at a gathering they are attending. Each kit includes the following:

- small crucifix
- Bible and stand
- pillar candle (battery operated)

- prayer cloths (actually, inexpensive place mats), one for each liturgical season: purple (Advent and Lent), green (Ordinary Time), white (Christmas and Easter)
- saint icon and stand
- CD with popular Catholic hymns

Armed with such a portable kit, prayer leaders can easily transform the setting of any parish gathering into a sacred space that is appropriate for worship. Now, let's move on to the notion of training prayer leaders to lead an experience of worship—which, I might add, is not rocket science. Prayer leaders do not perform; rather, they offer themselves as vehicles of the Spirit for those at prayer. In fact, being armed with a basic knowledge of the structure and elements of liturgical prayer will enable prayer leaders to function as such without reinventing the wheel each time they are called on to lead prayer. In general, liturgical prayer follows a basic pattern. Within that overall pattern, various elements are optional (except, I would argue, a proclamation from Scripture).

- Gathering/introduction—song, procession, greeting, opening prayer
- The word of God—Scripture reading(s), response, silence, song of meditation, spoken reflection
- Shared prayer—petitions/intercessions, traditional prayers, litanies, composed prayers
- Conclusion—closing prayer, blessing, song

You don't need to attend a two- or four-year lay ministry formation program to learn how to lead prayer. In fact, I have three free resources to offer on my blog—www.catechistsjourney.com—that any parish can use to help train people to be leaders of prayer.

- **Leading Prayer as a Catechist: A Webinar.** At the top of the home page of my blog, you'll find a tab for *Webinars*. Among the recorded webinars archived there is a one-hour webinar on how to lead others in prayer.

- **Simple Tips for Leading a Simple Prayer (Blog Post).** A while back, I offered a post on my blog under this title, which you can find by doing a simple search from the home page. In this post I provide an overview of what's involved in leading prayer, and then I offer the following:
- **Simple Tips for Leading a Simple Prayer (PDF).** You can download this PDF and use it as a primer for learning how to lead others in prayer.

Here's a bonus. I've written a two-page article, "Leading a Prayer Service: 16 Things to Consider," which you can find on the Loyola Press website—www.loyolapress.com. Just search the article title from the home page.

I have no doubt that a church on the move is a church that excels at worship. We need to stop saying perfunctory prayers at our gatherings and pray in a manner that is truly worship: a turning of our attention and energy to God, who alone sustains us.

———————

Worship is inscribed in the order of creation. As the rule of St. Benedict says, nothing should take precedence over "the work of God," that is, solemn worship. This indicates the right order of human concerns.
—Catechism of the Catholic Church, 347

Questions for Reflection and Discussion

- What are some things I do on a regular basis that are good for me?
- What are some of the benefits of worshipping God?
- What is the difference between saying a prayer and worshipping God?
- Outside of Sunday Mass, what other experiences of worship am I able to participate in?

Part Four

How a Church on the Move Forms Disciples in Faith

31

From Indoctrinating to Instigating

Catechesis . . . needs to go beyond simply the scholastic sphere to educate believers, from childhood, to meet Christ, living and working in his church.
—Pope Francis, audience, May 29, 2015

My wife, Joanne, who has been in the field of education since the early 1980s (she started when she was six years of age, of course!) tells me that a pet peeve of hers is hearing teachers introduce themselves as someone who teaches history, or science, or math, or English. She wants to say, "You don't teach history. You teach children." I have found myself wanting to say the same thing to catechists who tell me that they teach Old Testament, or Church history, or First Communion: "You don't teach church history. You teach children."

The fact is, we as a church are very doctrine driven. We talk about children "learning their catechism" by following a faith-formation curriculum arranged according to doctrinal areas:

Grade 1: God
Grade 2: First Reconciliation and First Eucharist
Grade 3: Church
Grade 4: Ten Commandments/Morality
Grade 5: The Seven Sacraments
Grade 6: Old Testament

Grade 7: Jesus/New Testament

Grade 8: Church History and/or Confirmation

I have nothing against doctrine. However, the fact remains that catechists are not teachers of a subject. Catechists are facilitators of an encounter with Jesus, who is *not* a subject. Jesus is a living Person who is present with us through the Holy Spirit. Our task is to introduce people to Jesus and to facilitate ever-deepening encounters with him. If we are to become a church on the move, we need to redesign our approach to faith formation so that it is not driven by doctrinal topics.

So now, here is a proposal for which I may lose my job!

OK, perhaps I'm exaggerating; however, I do work for a publishing company that provides two excellent basal faith-formation curricula: *Christ Our Life* and *Finding God*, both of which follow the doctrinal model described above. I am not suggesting that we do away with this doctrine. It can and should stay right where it is in the body of these textbooks. What should change, however, is the way we identify the theme of each year in religious education. Instead of identifying each year's theme as a doctrinal concept (here's what we believe), we should introduce each year according to works of mercy or, principles of Catholic social teaching (here's what we do). What might that look like? Here's an example.

Grade 1: Care for God's Creation

Grade 2: Feeding the Hungry and Giving Drink to the Thirsty

Grade 3: Call to Family, Community, Participation

Grade 4: Clothing the Naked

Grade 5: Sheltering the Homeless

Grade 6: Option for the Poor and Vulnerable

Grade 7: Visiting the Sick

Grade 8: Solidarity

The overriding goal of each year in faith formation would thus be to introduce young people to these works of mercy and to provide opportunities for them to practice these works of mercy by participating in what I call "mercy experiences" rather than "service projects." Within the context of these experiences of practicing mercy, we would continue to teach the traditional doctrinal content that is so vital to our identity as Catholics and that supports our relationship with the Trinity. What's different would be the lens through which we approach the doctrine. No longer would doctrine be seen as the overriding principle guiding that year of faith formation. Instead, faith formation would be powered by participating in experiences of sharing God's mercy and encountering Christ in those whom we serve.

When I was serving as a sixth-grade catechist several years ago at St. Cajetan parish on the south side of Chicago, I was thrilled to learn at my first catechist meeting that every grade—not just the confirmation class—was asked to do a service project with their kids. Together with my wife, who was serving as my aide that year, we arranged for young people to prepare and serve dinner for the current guests at Ronald McDonald House in Oak Lawn, near Advocate Christ Medical Center, a "home away from home" for families of children with complex medical needs. The young people dove into the experience with great enthusiasm and did a superb job of preparing and serving meals that evening. Months later, when I asked them to evaluate all that we had done in the past year in faith formation, including all the amazing lessons I had prepared and delivered to them (wink), the class unanimously voted their mercy experience at Ronald McDonald House their favorite experience in faith formation for the year.

As a child, I was taught to memorize the Corporal and Spiritual Works of Mercy. I was never given strategies or opportunities to actually practice those. If catechesis is truly to be an "apprenticeship in the whole Christian life," as the *General Directory for Catechesis* (63) refers to it, then we need to engage young people in the practices that embody our faith. Our Protestant brothers and sisters have been very good at doing this—involving young people in mission—as part of their faith formation, which is, perhaps, one of the reasons they seem to maintain a higher percentage of youth than the Catholic Church does. It isn't just because they provide more fun activities. It's because the young people feel that they are participating in a movement, not just learning concepts.

Earlier I spoke about the strategies employed by Communism to successfully "convert" one-third of the world's population in the first half of the twentieth century. One of those strategies was to put new recruits immediately into action. Teaching Communist doctrine came later; instigating a movement came first. If we are to become a church on the move, we need to relegate doctrine to its rightful role as part of the supporting cast and focus on creating instigators of God's mercy.

At the end of life we will not be judged by how many diplomas we have received, how much money we have made, how many great things we have done. We will be judged by "I was hungry, and you gave me something to eat, I was naked and you clothed me. I was homeless and you took me in."
—Blessed Mother Teresa

Questions for Reflection and Discussion

- Why is it not enough for our faith formation to be "doctrine driven"?

- What does it mean for our faith formation to be "mercy driven"?

- What "mercy experiences" have I participated in that have had an impact on me?

- What types of "mercy experiences" can young people engage in to get a true experience of apprenticeship in the Christian life?

32

From Child-Focused to Adult-Focused

Each (Catholic) community is "mature" when it professes faith, celebrates it with joy during the liturgy, lives charity, proclaims the Word of God endlessly, leaves its own to take it to the "peripheries," especially to those who have not yet had the opportunity to know Christ.

—Pope Francis, message for World Day of Peace, August 28, 2013

When I give talks about adult faith formation, I refuse to quote principles from the U.S. Bishops' document *Our Hearts Were Burning within Us.* That's not because I don't like the document. On the contrary, I consider it an outstanding document that makes a very clear case for the priority of adult catechesis. I refuse to quote principles from the document because we've been doing that for nearly two decades and not much has changed. So instead of spending time rehashing the principles from the document, I usually show a picture of the document in my slide presentation and tell my audience, "Read the darned thing!" For too long we've been giving lip service to this document without, for the most part, doing anything to change course in any significant way.

For an institution like the Catholic Church to change course is a mighty undertaking, especially when it comes to a well-oiled machine such as the one we've created to educate children. Organizations typically resist change. Many compare it to trying to change the course of a huge ocean liner, and we know what happened to the Titanic: by the time they noticed the problem, it was too late. I am confident that it is not too late for us as a church!

The larger, older, and slower an organization is, the harder it is to change course. Even the Hebrew people of the Old Testament, when faced with the uncertainties of their new life wandering the desert, yearned to return to the way things used to be when they were in slavery in Egypt. Change happens much more quickly in smaller, more-nimble organizations. The Catholic Church is neither small nor nimble. Newer organizations are more flexible and capable of change. The Catholic Church is not new. The world all around us is becoming accustomed to rapid change. The Catholic Church is not accustomed to moving quickly. Meanwhile, there are icebergs lurking all around us, threatening our ability to stay afloat. Perhaps the most serious threat to us is the reality that we are not doing a good job of forming adults into disciples of Christ. If we are going to become a church on the move, we need to make adult faith formation a real priority. No more lip service. In Charles Dickens's *A Christmas Carol*, Ebenezer Scrooge famously says, "Men's courses will foreshadow certain ends, to which, if persevered in, they must lead. . . . But if the courses be departed from, the ends will change." As a church, we must depart from the course we are on so that the ends will change.

So what can a parish do to begin turning the ship around? Begin with the following principle stated so accurately by my friend Nick Wagner: "Adults do *not* grow in faith by learning concepts." This means that the solution is not simply to provide more "classes" for adults. It means, rather, to look at everything the parish does through the lens of developing disciples. In other words, the parish must ask the question, *How does everything we do help adults deepen their friendship with God?* Each parish needs to sit down and identify what an adult who is fully formed in his or her faith looks like—without creating a portrait that is so idealistic that no human could ever attain it.

In simple terms, a fully formed adult Catholic is someone who sustains and expresses a relationship with Jesus through

- the ability to articulate a basic understanding of Catholic teachings;
- participation in the sacramental life of the church and an understanding of a language of mystery (sign, symbol, and ritual);
- living according to the moral principles required of a disciple of Christ;
- an active prayer life;
- participation in the life of the faith community; and
- commitment to the mission.

I recommend that every parish sit down with its staff and parish pastoral council and be brutally honest in answering the following questions.

A. What are all the ways we are currently helping adults grow in . . .

B. What are some of the ways we can help adults grow in . . .

1. knowledge of the faith?
2. knowledge of the meaning of the liturgy and the sacraments?
3. understanding what it means to live a moral life?
4. a life of prayer?

5. participation in the life of the community?

6. understanding what it means to have a missionary spirit?

In answering these questions, folks must resist the temptation to respond to question B by simply proposing more classes. Rather, creative approaches need to be explored: online initiatives, small groups, social media, and print materials, for starters. The remainder of this unit is dedicated to exploring some of these creative options and avenues for engaging adults in faith formation beyond inviting them to sit and listen to a lecture. However, it all begins with a commitment to making this a parish priority.

Adult faith formation is not accomplished via a program or an event or even a series of events. Rather, it is stimulated by a wide variety of approaches that ultimately lead to a "change of climate" in the parish—one in which adult faith formation is fostered at every turn. When it comes to adult faith formation, you had better become a believer in climate change, because that's what is required: we need to create a climate in our parishes that fosters the growth of adult faith.

Catechesis for adults, since it deals with persons who are capable of an adherence that is fully responsible, must be considered the chief form of catechesis. All the other forms, which are indeed always necessary, are in some way oriented to it.
—General Directory for Catechesis, 59

Questions for Reflection and Discussion

How is my parish helping me grow in . . .

How can my parish help me grow in . . .

- knowledge of the faith?
- knowledge of the meaning of the liturgy and the sacraments?
- understanding what it means to live a moral life?
- a life of prayer?
- participation in the life of the community?
- understanding what it means to have a missionary spirit?

33

From Complex to Simple

---

*Without the grammar of simplicity, the church loses the very
conditions which make it possible "to fish" for God in the deep
waters of his Mystery.*
—Pope Francis to Brazilian Bishops, July 27, 2013

A priest friend of mine shares a story about visiting his niece and
catching a glimpse of all the massive textbooks she would be
required to read for her high school senior-year classes: literature, science, history, and language. He then noticed that her religion "text-
book" was very thin and filled with what he described as cartoonish
illustrations, large print, and neon colors. In essence, he says, it was a
comic book. The priest uses that story to illustrate what he calls the
"dumbing down" of the Catholic faith, and he laments the fact that
his niece's required reading for religion did not include classics of our
Catholic heritage such as Augustine, Aquinas, Chesterton, Theresa
of Avila, Flannery O'Connor, C. S. Lewis, and more (copies all of
which he purchased for his niece to read on her own).

While our young people deserve much more than a comic book
for religion class, I do not agree with my friend's suggestion that
the solution to the religious illiteracy of many Catholics today is
to intellectualize our approach to faith formation. When I was in
high school, I studied many great classics of literature, including

Shakespeare, Chaucer, Dickens, and the Brontë sisters, but developed no desire to pursue the classics any further, although I continue to appreciate them from a distance. My point is, the solution to what some call the "dumbing down" of Catholicism is not to overcompensate with a highly intellectualized approach to Catholicism. The pendulum, unfortunately, seems to swing from one extreme to the other, and neither extreme is the solution. Catholicism is not all head, nor is it all heart. It is both head and heart. I don't know what "comic books" my friend's niece used for her senior-year religion class, but they certainly don't sound adequate. Dumbing down the Catholic faith is the wrong approach. However, so is over-intellectualizing it. Our goal should be to make the Catholic faith accessible, and we can accomplish that by making it simple, not simplistic.

In the early 1960s, the United States Navy adopted the acronym KISS—Keep It Simple, Stupid—as a guiding principle for their engineers. Recognizing that their systems would need to be repaired by average mechanics in combat zones without the presence of expert engineers, the Navy insisted that they be kept simple. In a similar way, our doctrines and theology need to be accessible to the average person to apply in everyday living without the presence of expert theologians to assist them. Doctrine, in fact, is not intended for theologians; it is intended to assist everyday people in articulating the mystery of God, who is encountered in everyday living. Most Catholics, unfortunately, have assumed that doctrines and theology are above their pay grade and should best be left to expert theologians. With the *Catechism of the Catholic Church* "weighing in" at over 900 pages, this should come as no surprise; it does not fit easily into one's hip pocket or handbag. Theology that is too dense and complex suggests that God is not easily accessible, which is counterproductive to proclaiming the nearness of God.

And yet the Catholic faith rests on only four pillars: creed, sacraments, morality, and prayer. Even our Muslim brothers and sisters have five pillars—we've got it easy compared to them! In my book *A Well-Built Faith: A Catholic's Guide to Knowing and Sharing What We Believe*, I propose an acronym to help Catholics remember these four pillars: HELP.

> H—We HOLD onto the beliefs of our faith in the creed.
> E—We EXPRESS our faith in the sacraments and worship.
> L—We LIVE our faith through a moral life.
> P—We PRAY our faith through a life of prayer.

If we are going to be a church on the move, we've got to keep it simple. This is the advice that Pope Emeritus Benedict XVI gave to an audience of priests when one of them asked him to impart some wisdom about catechesis. Benedict said, "Let us not lose the simplicity of the truth" (Question and Answer Session with Parish Priests, February 26, 2009). Of all people, Pope Emeritus Benedict XVI would never encourage us to make the Catholic faith simplistic. He did, however, recognize that much of our doctrinal vocabulary is incomprehensible to today's world. That doesn't mean that we jettison it, but it does mean that we need to translate it. We accomplish this by keeping it simple when introducing people to Jesus Christ. We don't need to go to distant lands to find people who have yet to encounter Christ—they are in our midst, and in many if not most cases, our proclamation of the Good News to them must be considered an "initial" proclamation, even if folks have technically been catechized and sacramentalized. Unless we keep things simple, our proclamation of the Good News will be like sowing seeds in soil that has not been tilled.

A Well-Built Faith, which is a simple, accessible introduction to the four pillars of the Catholic faith, is no substitute for the

Catechism of the Catholic Church. Rather, it is intended to whet the appetite for deeper knowledge (head and heart) of God that will lead people to explore more complex presentations of the Catholic faith, such as the *Catechism.* I sincerely hope that, after reading my books, Catholics will develop a desire to read books by more complex thinkers and from there will move on to reading Catholic classics such as Aquinas, Chesterton, and Teresa of Ávila.

In my presentations I often tell my audience that if they were asked to give an overview of the Catholic faith to someone, they would receive a satisfactory grade if they recited the creed, described the seven sacraments, named the Ten Commandments, and said the Lord's Prayer. Is there more to the Catholic faith? Of course. But for starters, these are the four basic pillars of our faith. If we are going to be a church on the move, we're going to have to learn how to keep it simple.

Simplicity is the ultimate sophistication.
—attributed to Leonardo da Vinci

Questions for Reflection and Discussion

- Who taught the Catholic faith to me in a way that made it accessible? Who "kept it simple" for me?
- What Catholic classics have I read? When, in my spiritual journey, did I read these, and how did they affect me?
- How would I describe the four pillars of the Catholic faith to someone?
- What can parishes do to "keep it simple" when proclaiming the Catholic faith?

34

From Parents as Chauffeurs to Parents as Catechists

It is time for fathers and mothers to return from their exile—for they have exiled themselves from their children's upbringing—and to fully resume their educational role.
—Pope Francis, General Audience, May 20, 2015

Over the past century, the church has wrongly convinced parents that their only duty in their children's faith formation is to chauffeur them. As a result, we have cultivated a drop-off mentality among parents that we are now struggling to break. This is not a criticism of parents. The church has trained parents to do this. We have done a great job of placing few to no expectations on parents when it comes to the faith formation of their children. In truth, the drop-off model for religious education worked extremely well back in the day when children grew up in what I call "Catholic bubbles." Up until the 1960s, Catholics tended to live together in tight-knit communities, where Catholicism was lived and breathed. The vast majority of kids in the neighborhood attended the Catholic school, and the unfortunate souls who didn't—the "publics"—went to CCD class to learn their catechism. Either way, you learned your faith mostly by osmosis: you simply soaked it in from the family and the community, which oozed Catholicism. In essence, the community formed young people in faith. All that was needed was the memorization of some Catholic vocabulary and doctrinal formulas, and parents were happy to drop off their kids to get that.

I need not remind you that it is now the twenty-first century. We don't live in Catholic bubbles anymore. And yet we are still using the same model for religious education that succeeded in the 1950s as long as parents got the kids to class.

If we are going to be a church on the move, we have to change our approach, and fast.

Pope Francis has made it clear that parents need to take a more active role in their children's faith formation, saying it's time for their "exile" to end. One person who is an effective voice for empowering parents to form their children in faith in cooperation with the parish is Patrice Spirou, Assistant Director for Religious Education for the Archdiocese of Atlanta, who has been a religious educator for more than twenty years. As a DRE in a parish in the Diocese of Joliet, she initiated a parish family-centered catechesis program, which grew from forty-six to more than four hundred families in a few short years. Parents gathered with their kids at the parish once per month for an intergenerational experience that equipped and empowered them to teach the remaining lessons for the month at home. With almost six hundred adults in attendance each month, it unwittingly evolved into the largest adult faith-formation program in the diocese. Patrice explains: "Such enormous growth is a clear testament to the fact that something had to change in the way we ministered to families. In fact, the response from parents revealed there was a hunger for learning and growth for the whole family! It was time for a new focus, a new approach. Family life has changed, and we as a church need to adapt to those changes to meet our people where they are in order to effectively minister to them. In this moment, families are poised, hoping to finally be seen, heard, and fed according to their needs, not ours."

Here is what a family-centered approach to catechesis might look like.

- Parents and their children come together for a monthly session at the parish.
- The experience begins with parents and children together in one location for an introduction and a prayer experience.
- Catechists then lead students (perhaps in procession?) to their age-appropriate classrooms for grade-level instruction on the opening chapter of a unit.
- At the same time, parents participate in exploring these same concepts through adult presentations and discussions.
- Parents are equipped with knowledge and resources not to only deepen their own friendship with God but also to work on the remaining unit chapters with their children at home throughout the month.
- At the end of each monthly session, parents are dismissed to the classrooms to pick up their children. (Some traditional weekly religious-education programs have taken to requiring parents to enter the building to pick up their children so that parents have some interaction with catechists.)
- In the weeks that follow, parents work with their children at home on the remaining chapters of the unit. Some publishers now provide at-home guides to assist parents in teaching their children the faith.
- Children complete and turn in an assessment at the end of each unit to determine how well they comprehend the concepts being taught; this is a measure of accountability to ensure that lessons are indeed taking place at home.

Making the change from a traditional religious education program with a drop-off mentality to a family catechesis model requires a great deal of planning and educating of parents to adjust to the new model. Even then, some parents will be angry that they are being forced to teach their children, because they have been trained to believe that this responsibility belongs to the parish. Some will leave. If you commit to empowering them to form their children in faith, most parents will respond positively and will come to a new appreciation of their own faith formation. Finally, embracing this new model requires a huge letting go—to trust that parents are indeed working with their kids at home on their lessons. We must remember, however, that the present traditional structure of religious education also has huge risks involved—namely, trusting that what we teach kids in an hour each week will "stick" with little or no parental involvement or support the rest of the week. All the evidence shows that this is not working for us.

To be a church on the move, we need to equip parents to embrace their role as the primary educators of their children in the faith. No other vehicle can communicate the nearness of God as effectively as the family.

It is for this reason that the Christian community must give very special attention to parents. By means of personal contact, meetings, courses and also adult catechesis directed toward parents, the Christian community must help them assume their responsibility—which is particularly delicate today—of educating their children in the faith.
—General Directory for Catechesis, 227

Questions for Reflection and Discussion

- What role did my parents play in my faith formation? What role have I had in my children's faith formation?
- Why is the drop-off approach to religious education no longer working?
- What do I see as the benefits of a family-centered approach to catechesis?
- What kind of support do parents need if this model is to be truly effective?

35

From One-Size-Fits-All to Variety

To be sure, the testimony of faith comes in very many forms, just as in a great fresco, there is a variety of colours and shades; yet they are all important, even those that do not stand out.
—Pope Francis, homily for the Mass in the Basilica of St. Paul Outside the Walls, April 14, 2013

In the past several decades, the weight of the average American has increased by more than twenty pounds. Yikes! It's no wonder that clothing rarely comes in "one-size-fits-all" as it once did. There's no way that one size can stretch far enough to cover all of our various shapes and sizes.

Too often, parishes approach adult faith formation with a one-size-fits-all mentality, as though it were simply the adult version of children's religious education, taking place on a given date and time and with a given topic. If you can make it, fine. If not, oh well. Thus, parishes with several thousand families are content with the fact that they had forty-three people at their last adult faith formation session—up from thirty-seven. That's fine, but what about the other few thousand?

If we are going to be a church on the move, we need to do away with the one-size-fits-all approach to adult faith formation. When speaking about variety in adult faith formation, I'm not suggesting that we simply repeat the one program we have on different days of the week or at different times or that we multiply the number of topics covered within the same format. Adult faith formation needs to take on many different shapes and genres, so to speak, and they need not, nor should they, look like "classes." So what do I mean by different shapes and genres? Here are some examples:

- **Local pilgrimages.** Arrange to take groups to various locations on day trips to visit and experience sacred and historical sites that teach us about our faith. One pastor I spoke to said he thoroughly enjoys the bus rides for such local pilgrimages because he can really sit and talk to people for significant periods of time as opposed to the quick greetings that take place outside the church after Mass on Sundays. Local pilgrimages often attract people who may not be attending church but are interested in some aspect of the site you are visiting, thus making it an evangelizing opportunity.

- **Book discussion groups.** Arrange for groups to meet in homes or at restaurants or coffee shops to read and discuss various books that deepen and enrich our faith. Again, some people may be drawn to reading a book before they are drawn to attending church.

- **Mentoring relationships.** Arrange for more experienced Catholics to mentor newer Catholics in Catholic practices. While many people feel ill-equipped to explain doctrines, many Catholics are much more comfortable talking about Catholic practices. This is especially helpful for those in the role of sponsor for the RCIA or confirmation.

- **Marriage enrichment dinners.** Arrange for Catholic married couples to gather occasionally/regularly for dinner at a restaurant, followed by a speaker and discussion about issues related to nurturing a faith-filled marriage. If we really want to support the institution of marriage, we need to offer ongoing opportunities for married people to gather and reflect on their relationship as it grows and endures challenges that come along throughout life.

- **Small faith-sharing groups.** Arrange for small groups of ten to fifteen to meet in homes to read, pray, reflect, and discuss the weekly Scripture readings. (See chapter 39.) Even though I am not a betting man, I would easily wager that a parish with ten small groups, each consisting of twelve people gathering weekly, would never be able to gather all 120 of those people on one evening at the parish for a single event. Jesus multiplied the loaves—he didn't make one huge loaf!

- **Online learning initiatives.** Arrange for parishioners to participate in an online faith-formation experience that extends over several weeks. Gather folks together to kick it off and again to bring it to a close, but allow most of the learning to take place at home at people's convenience.

- **Links to YouTube videos.** Arrange to e-mail all parishioners a weekly link to a brief but substantive and engaging/informative YouTube video by a reliable Catholic source that helps parishioners grow in knowledge of the faith.

- **Catechesis at existing parish meetings.** Arrange for each group or organization in the parish (women's club, men's club, finance committee, parish pastoral council) to include ten minutes of catechesis at their regular meetings. The parish can ask each organization to call forth one or two members to be the group's catechist(s) and then can work with these individuals to help them find resources to conduct mini-catechetical sessions their groups that already meet regularly at the parish to conduct business.

- **Catechetical service events/opportunities.** Arrange for parishioners to participate in occasional major service events such as building a home for Habitat for Humanity or Catholic

Relief Services' Helping Hands project (a meal-packaging program), and include faith formation as part of the overall experience. This can also be done with ongoing human-concerns efforts, which often take place apart from prayer and catechetical input.

These examples just scratch the surface. Think outside the box, or at least outside the classroom. Drop the lecture and get creative in your approaches to adult faith formation. If we are going to be a church on the move, we need to get more creative in our approaches to adult faith formation and do away with the one-size-fits-all approach, which does not work.

Given the broad scope of content, the diverse range of adult interests and responsibilities, and the availability of learning resources, no single approach can meet everyone's needs. Consequently, a comprehensive, multi-faceted, and coordinated approach to adult faith formation is necessary.
—*Our Hearts Were Burning within Us*, 98

Questions for Reflection and Discussion

- Why should adult faith-formation opportunities not look like "classes"?
- What unique and creative genres for adult faith formation can I think of to add to the list in this chapter?
- Why do our adult faith offerings need to be less "churchy" sounding?
- What "outside-the-box" faith formation opportunities have I experienced?

36

From Passive Pupils to Empowered Faith Sharers

Let us not forget that the Apostles were simple people; they were neither scribes nor doctors of the law, nor did they belong to the class of priests. With their limitations and with the authorities against them, how did they manage to fill Jerusalem with their teaching?
—Pope Francis, Regina Coeli, April 14, 2013

Think about the people in the pews in your parish, including yourself. What do these folks do all day? They run companies, manage departments and teams, do sales presentations and training programs, run households, oversee programs and logistics, and perform any number of other skilled tasks. Each of these folks excels in various areas and exhibits skills and competencies pertaining to his or her areas of expertise. For whatever reason, however, when they come to church for any kind of formation, we tend to treat them like children. We condescendingly invite them into a passive mode while one of the "experts" on the parish staff or a guest speaker pontificates over the proceedings. The overall dynamic is one of a "sage on the stage" delivering content to passive pupils in the audience.

Shame on us. It is no wonder that among the reasons people give for leaving the church, according to author Josh Packard in *Church Refugees: Sociologists Reveal Why People Are Done with Church but Not Their Faith*, is the feeling that they are fed up with "prepackaged lectures" and the "predetermined conclusions" of parish speakers and leaders. They are accustomed to arriving at conclusions on their own after grappling with them and engaging in dialogue with others as opposed to being told what to think and believe. This does not mean that adult faith formation is "anything goes." It does mean, however, engaging people in mature conversation that leads them to discover together the truths God has revealed to us.

In a parish where I was invited to assist in growing adult faith formation, the pastor told me that most of their gatherings for parents of children in the school and religious education programs had been disastrous up until that point. Such meetings were kept as short as possible (forty-five minutes maximum) because people resented their time being taken up by information that could have been sent out easily via e-mail. As we set out to alter the culture in the parish and invite adults to gatherings in which they might encounter Christ, the pastor and others warned me that folks would be taken aback and that they were not accustomed to speaking to one another about their faith. I totally get that. We Catholics have been taught about our faith while rarely being invited to share our faith with others.

For the very first attempt—a parent meet-and-greet with the religious education catechists—we put our heads together to shape an experience in which adults would be welcomed into a meaningful prayer experience (not just the perfunctory Hail Mary or Our Father). This was followed by an invitation to engage in some very nonthreatening conversation at their tables—more of an icebreaker than any intense faith-sharing—before the parents met the catechists. To facilitate this, we used the conversation-starter cards from a product called *The Meal Box* by Bret Nicholaus and Tom McGrath: fifty-four cards with questions designed to begin conversations around the dinner table or in other settings. Here are some sample questions.

- If someone gave you a thousand dollars in cash—in the form of ten hundred-dollar bills—and told you that you had to give it all away within twenty-four hours, to whom would you give the money?
- As best you can remember, what has been the most exciting moment in your life to this point?
- If you had to wear an object around your neck at all times, something that would be attached to a thick chain or string, what would it be? (Don't choose something too heavy—you have to wear it all the time!)
- Almost everyone, adults included, has a favorite place in their mind to go to when they need to get away from reality for a moment or two. What is your favorite place to day-dream about?

For people who are not accustomed to sharing faith with one another, this is an inviting way to welcome them to begin to open up a little to others. Over time, folks can be invited to share at a deeper level, but it is important not to come on too strong at first. Faith sharing at a deeper level might look something like this. I once had the pleasure of observing a confirmation sponsor-candidate meeting facilitated by my friend Bob Burnham at a parish on the south side of Chicago. I enjoyed watching as Bob provided brief chunks of solid theological background on three topics (fifteen to twenty minutes each) and facilitated three meaningful conversations between the candidates and their sponsors (ten minutes each) on the topics, truly honoring the role of the sponsor as someone leading an apprentice on a faith journey. Specifically, Bob invited the confirmation candidates and their sponsors to engage in meaningful conversation about the following three topics/questions:

1. **Becoming DO-ERS of the Word.** Candidates, what do you like to do? What are your gifts and talents? How can you use these to set goals for your life? Sponsors, how can you help your candidate reach these goals?

2. **Gifts of the Holy Spirit/Saint Examples.** Sponsors, which gift would you like to share with your candidate? How would you share it? Candidates, which gift do you see and admire in your sponsor?

3. **Bringing Grace to Others.** Candidates, complete the following sentences: I use my talents and gifts to serve God and others by . . . / I see God in . . . / I bring out the best in people by . . . / The person I look to the most for help is . . .

Rather than just deliver a lecture to confirmation candidates and their sponsors, Bob facilitated an evening in which sponsors were empowered to do what they are called to do: mentor their candidates. If we are going to be a church on the move, we can no longer treat adults like passive pupils. Rather, we need to invite, equip, and empower them to take ownership of their own formation and to share faith and wisdom with one another instead of making them think that it has to come solely from an expert. In doing so, they more quickly come to develop an ever-deepening awareness of God's nearness and their own desirability in God's eyes.

Adult catechesis should respect the experience of adults and make use of their personal experiences, skills, and talents.
—National Directory for Catechesis, 48.A.4

Questions for Reflection and Discussion

- As I think of three or four adult friends and their professions, can I identify how they exhibit expertise and leadership in their positions? How could these skills be better respected in adult faith settings?
- What difference would it make to have a panel of parishioners "share the stage" with a presenter at adult faith-formation events?
- When have I felt as though I were being treated like a passive pupil at an adult faith-formation event? How can this be rectified?
- What examples from the gospels can I identify in which Jesus taught by engaging people in conversation? What can I learn from Jesus' approach?

37

From Creating Quasi Clerics to Training Leaders and Facilitators

---

At this time of crisis we cannot be concerned solely with ourselves, withdrawing into loneliness, discouragement and a sense of powerlessness in the face of problems. Please do not withdraw into yourselves!
—Pope Francis, May 8, 2013

Leaders are people who are not concerned solely with themselves. They are dedicated to the betterment of others. A church on the move needs leaders. Of course, we already have leaders: our magisterium, our pastors, and our lay ecclesial ministers. However, we need more leaders within the parish—leaders who can facilitate the faith formation of countless small faith-sharing groups.

Unfortunately, when it comes to forming lay leaders in the parish, the church seems to insist that their formation resemble seminary training: multiyear programs that are heavily theological, thus running the risk of creating quasi clerics and a new type of clericalism. The most pressing need in developing parishes that evangelize is not to form mini-theologians with few relational skills but rather to empower effective leaders and facilitators to animate groups of people in sharing faith. Leadership training of lay leaders should never be divorced from spirituality; neither should it be heavily theological. And such training must not overtax the schedules of laypeople, who must work within the time constraints of jobs and family life.

Small-group leaders and facilitators are not teachers, experts, advisors, theologians, or problem solvers. To facilitate means "to make easy." They simply rely on certain skills and techniques to enable a small faith group to run smoothly. Most important, to facilitate means to place yourself in the service of others just as Jesus taught us to serve. So just what are the qualities needed in a facilitator of a small faith group? A small-group facilitator is someone who . . .

- is practicing his or her faith and is a good listener;
- possesses common sense and is not overly sensitive;
- is a team player and a people person and possesses empathy, warmth, and genuineness; and
- has a tolerance for differing opinions and is open to diversity.

Leadership training should aim at equipping parishioners to do the following:

Preparations and Hospitality

- The role of the leader/facilitator begins before anyone even arrives: making preparations and looking over the plan for the gathering so that it will flow well.
- Just as a wait staff prepares a dining room for a banquet, leaders prepare the environment in which the small group will gather, paying attention to seating arrangements (avoiding a lecture or classroom arrangement) and arranging a space that communicates the sacred in our midst: a table with a Bible, a candle, a crucifix, and any other sacred objects that are appropriate for the gathering.

- Leaders make sure that refreshments and hospitality are offered.
- Effective leaders never underestimate the importance of signage, especially at the beginning, so that people can find their way to the gathering with ease.
- Leaders welcome people as they arrive, greet them personally and make them feel at home, introduce people to one another, provide name tags as needed, and invite group members to enjoy refreshments and to socialize.

Facilitation and Leading Discussion

- Once everyone has arrived and had a chance to socialize, the job of a leader/facilitator is to call people to get down to business. The leader sets the tone in a pleasant and inviting manner and invites people to focus on the task at hand.
- Leaders set the tone by leading the group in a prayer experience.
- Leaders and facilitators must be aware that adults
    - are self-motivated (they resist ideas being imposed) and bring life experience that must be respected;
    - are goal-oriented (they learn in order to cope with life transitions and want to apply immediately what they have learned) and demand relevance and practicality and need to take ownership;
    - have time commitments that must be respected, and they learn best in relational, interactive, conversational settings; and
    - like to laugh!
- Leaders guide discussion, learning to
    - limit their own talking and find a balance between being controlling at one extreme and unassertive at the other;

- ° affirm others' comments, listen, and stay attentive;
- ° invite quiet types to share their thoughts and politely interrupt those who dominate the conversation;
- ° gently bring the discussion back to focus if a tangent occurs and ask for clarification if someone's statement or point is unclear.

- Leaders also learn how to effectively ask questions by
  - ° phrasing questions in a simple, straightforward way and keeping questions open-ended;
  - ° remaining comfortable with silence when awaiting a response;
  - ° planning questions ahead of time, asking a question of the whole group first, pausing, and repeating it; and
  - ° refraining from answering their own questions
  - ° giving feedback/affirmation to participants when they respond to questions.

Handling Challenges and Various Responsibilities

- Part of the job of a facilitator is to handle difficult participants. Leaders learn to deal with dominators, shy types, tangent makers, and antagonists, often by speaking to problem participants individually before or after a session to ask them to make some adjustments to their behavior.

- Finally, leaders and facilitators learn to do the following:
  - ° Call members who were absent to check up on them.
  - ° Send people home with additional resources when appropriate.
  - ° Summarize the gathering.
  - ° Promise to gather information in response to a question no one could answer.
  - ° End with prayer.

I provide a Leadership Training slide presentation (with script) on my blog, which you can access, at no cost, by going to this link: http://bit.ly/1NUfWz0.

Serving as a small-group facilitator is an opportunity to help others recognize and encounter Christ, who is in our midst and who walks with us on our journey. A church on the move recognizes that the Holy Spirit is the true facilitator and guide but develops leaders and facilitators to cooperate with the Spirit's movements and to remove obstacles that prohibit small groups from truly encountering Christ.

This demands a change in mindset, particularly concerning lay people. They must no longer be viewed as "collaborators" of the clergy but truly recognized as "co-responsible" for the church's being and action, thereby fostering the consolidation of a mature and committed laity.
—Pope Benedict XVI, Opening of the Pastoral Convention of the Diocese of Rome, May 26, 2009

Questions for Reflection and Discussion

- Who are good leaders in my parish? Who would make good leaders?
- In my experience of participating in small groups, whether at church or in other venues, what skills have I noticed as important if a leader is to facilitate effectively?
- What could my parish accomplish with an "army" of well-trained leaders and facilitators? What ministries might be able to begin and flourish?
- What skills and qualities do I bring to the role of leader/facilitator?

38

From Hoping the "Nones" Come Back to Strategizing Their Retention

---

*Dear young men and women, in Christ you find fulfilled your
every desire for goodness and happiness. He alone can satisfy
your deepest longings, which are so often clouded by deceptive
worldly promises.*
—Pope Francis, message for the 30th World Youth Day,
January 31, 2015

I don't know about you, but I'm tired of hearing about the Nones:
those folks—primarily young adults—who indicate "None" when
surveyed about their denominational affiliation and who now,
alarmingly, constitute a larger percentage of the population in the
United States than Catholics (Pew Research Center, Religious Landscape Study, 2015). I know this is a very serious problem, so when
I say that I'm sick of hearing about the Nones, I'm not suggesting
that we just bury our heads in the sand and hope the problem will
go away. I'm tired of hearing all the talk about the Nones because
I'm not hearing much in the way of practical ideas for addressing
the problem, and those ideas that I do hear overlook perhaps the
most major need facing young adults as they go through college and
beyond—namely, survival.

Young adults, loaded down with student loans and other pressing economic realities, are in need of income. They need jobs. They simply cannot be bothered with church and the condition of their immortal souls when they don't know what tomorrow holds. According to *U.S. News & World Report*, nearly seventy percent of graduating seniors leave college with a financial burden averaging $30,000. In the United States, youth unemployment (among sixteen- to twenty-four-year-olds) is nearly twice the national rate (U.S. Department of Labor Bureau of Labor Statistics), while in some countries, such as Spain, it is at an alarming rate of fifty percent.

So what should we do about it? We should give them jobs.

I'm dead serious. What college-age student wouldn't "die" for a paid internship over the summer? A few thousand bucks to help pay some bills, maybe buy a used car, maybe even save a little. I'm proposing that Catholic parishes offer paid internships to college-age students during the summer months when they are home from school. And what would these internships be in? Faith formation. We would pay them to intern as catechists during the summer, training and forming them as they simultaneously serve as catechists for summer intensive catechetical sessions for elementary-grade students. Here's what it might look like.

- Parishes would commit to offering between six and twelve internships (perhaps more for parishes with larger budgets).
- The internships should be named after someone who represents the parish legacy, and they should be presented as a prestigious parish honor.
- The internships would be for six weeks, beginning in June when college students return home and lasting until the end of July, in time for students to prepare to return to college in August.

- The internships would pay somewhere in the area of $2,500 per intern.
- The parish staff would actively identify young adults they feel would be the best fit for the experience and would invite them to apply.
- The application would include an essay explaining why they feel they should be considered for these internships.
- The internships should be awarded at a Sunday Mass, and the assembly should commission the interns and pray over them at that time.
- The interns would begin an intensive course of study (cate-chetical methodology/pedagogy and theological formation) leading to their certification as catechists. Parishes could cluster together regionally to provide staff to teach the courses.
- The first two weeks of the internship would be solely training and formation along with practice teaching. Prayer and liturgy would be major components of the program.
- The next three weeks of the program would involve the interns in serving as catechists for a summer intensive cate-chetical session for elementary-grade students. Faith formation programs such as Loyola Press's *Finding God* and *Christ Our Life* include models for a three-week summer intensive. A summer intensive program for faith formation enables a parish to focus on intergenerational faith-formation events throughout the "academic year" as well as involve young people in works of mercy—service experiences—and weekly Liturgy of the Word for children.
- Each day after teaching, the interns would continue with an abbreviated schedule of training and formation.
- The final week of the internship, after the summer intensive has ended, would return to intensive formation to complete

certification as catechists according to local diocesan standards.

- At the end of the internship, the interns should be presented with the catechist certificates at Sunday Mass, thanked, and prayed over as they prepare to head back to school.

For centuries and for millions of people around the world, Christianity has long been seen as a way to a better life. In many blighted areas, young people have found a way out of poverty by entering convents and seminaries, not as a type of welfare but as a true opportunity to discover their own gifts and use them to bring relief to others who are suffering. In other words, such examples are perfect descriptions of the difference between giving people a fish so that they can eat for a day and teaching them to fish so that they can eat for a lifetime. Catechetical internships for young people address a critical issue facing us today: the increasing pressure on young adults to get their economic footing.

An ancient proverb says that "an empty belly has no ears." Our young people today may not literally have empty bellies; however, their empty bank accounts prevent them from having the ears they need to hear the Good News. The catechetical internship approach addresses this reality, not by treating young people as helpless but, rather, by empowering them to begin taking steps toward their own economic independence while at the same time enabling them to discover their gifts, deepen their faith, and become "people for others." We will not be able to become a church on the move unless we have young people who can get behind and push.

Business underlies everything in our national life, including our spiritual life. Witness the fact that in the Lord's Prayer, the first petition is for daily bread. No one can worship God or love his neighbor on an empty stomach.
—Woodrow Wilson, Speech in New York, May 23, 1912

Questions for Reflection and Discussion

- What have I heard, in conversation or in research and reports, about the reality of "Nones"?
- What do I see as the reasons for so many young people identifying themselves as having no religious affiliation?
- If my parish had paid internships for young people in the area of faith formation, whom might the award be named after? Why?
- Who are some young adults I know who are in "survival mode" right now—coping with student debt and little or no cash flow? Of these, who might serve a paid internship in faith formation? What qualities should these interns possess to qualify?

39

From Impersonal Parish to Small Faith-Sharing Communities

It is in our brothers and sisters, with their gifts and limitations
that [the Lord] comes to meet us and make himself known. This
is what it means to belong to the Church.
—Pope Francis, General Audience, June 25, 2014

It is quite characteristic of human beings to join with others in groups. Instinctively, we discovered the need to join groups in order to survive. In general, human beings form groups in order to accomplish goals. Beyond that, however, is the fact that we are compelled to seek acceptance from our peers, and groups provide that opportunity. In search of that acceptance, people join a variety of groups: Scouts, book clubs, chess clubs, bowling leagues, Facebook groups, local softball teams, local gangs, and even terrorist cells. When it comes to experiencing that sense of acceptance in a group, less is more. In other words, people in small groups have a better chance of forming relationships that will truly benefit them. Likewise, the larger a group gets, the less an individual may feel that his or her contribution will have an impact.

One of the reasons we are having trouble becoming a church on the move is that we are simply getting too big. According to the

Center for Applied Research in the Apostolate, the overall size of parishes in the U.S. grew by over thirty-five percent in the first ten years of this century. People are finding it difficult to get a true sense of belonging in parishes that are becoming increasingly impersonal. This may lead you to question why megachurches such as Willow Creek and Saddleback Church, with tens of thousands of worshippers, continue to attract people in droves. The truth is, they combat the dangers of size by offering small-group experiences based on their belief that nothing has the power to change lives as effectively as a small group.

It is important to remember that most of Jesus' teaching took place in small groups. Likewise, the early church, under the guidance of the Holy Spirit, met in small groups in people's homes to pray together, to share meals, to worship, and to study the teachings of the apostles. Today, for us to truly be a church on the move, followers of Jesus must gather in small groups to pray, to share faith, and to learn the good news of Jesus. For small groups to be successful, they need the leadership of a facilitator.

Forming small faith-sharing groups in the parish is not as complex as one may think. Several years ago an average middle-class Catholic parish in Chicago, St. Barnabas Parish (1,600 registered families; about 5,300 individuals), created small faith-sharing groups for the first time in its parish history and successfully shepherded 200 parishioners (meeting weekly for ninety minutes in homes) into the small-group experience during Lent.

The success of the efforts at St. Barnabas is grounded in the fact that the parish did not simply purchase a "canned" program but, rather, developed a process that was suited to the needs of that parish community. The end result was an initiative they named "Companions on the Journey." Here are the first steps toward successfully planning and implementing small faith groups in your parish.

4–6 Months Out

- Assign a staff coordinator for the initiative.
- Gather (assemble if needed) the parish adult faith-formation commission/team to serve as the animating/organizing body for the initiative.
- With that team, define the mission, goals, and objectives for a successful initiative.
- Identify which staff members will be needed for the initiative, and define their participation and responsibilities.
- Establish a budget policy for the initiative—which department's budget, or which category of budget, absorbs the costs for kickoff and promotional materials, participant resources, etc.
- Define team and individual roles, along with brief descriptions for those roles; staff "buy in" is essential for success.

2–3 Months Out

- Research and select discussion materials your groups will use.
- Prepare a list of potential small-group leaders and host homes. Staff should participate in this recommendation-and-recruitment process because they have relationships within the ministries and organizations they direct.
- Mail an invitation to recommended leaders.
- Acquire facilitator training resources. (See chapter 37.)
- Follow up on facilitator invitation letters, by phone or in person.
- Plan a leadership training session.

1–2 Months Out

- Conduct leadership/facilitator training. (See chapter 37.)
- Prepare bulletin articles introducing the Lenten small faith groups.

- Prepare promotional materials such as posters, fliers, etc.

1 Month Out

- Prepare intercessions for the two weeks leading up to Sign-Up Sunday and the Sundays of Lent.
- Prepare priests to speak from the pulpit about the small faith groups.
- Begin bulletin announcements.
- Include information and sign-up options online, through the parish Web site.
- Display promotional materials (posters, signs).
- Host Sign-Up Sunday.
- Begin pulpit announcements.
- Include relevant intercessions in the Prayers of the Faithful.
- Collect final registrations.
- Assign participants to small groups.
- Give leaders their group rosters.
- Send participants notification of assigned meeting day/time/address.

Throughout Lent

- Invite participants to submit reflections on the experience of their small groups, to be shared in the bulletin and on the parish Web site.
- Provide bulletin inserts related to the Sunday Scripture.
- Invite the parish to pray for the small groups through intercessions at Mass and in their personal prayer.
- Invite others to join groups.

Several Weeks after Easter

- Host a closing celebration with Mass and a potluck dinner.
- Invite participants to evaluate the experience.

- Invite small groups to continue meeting if they so desire, and provide them with resources for faith sharing.

In the Foreword to the book *Small Groups with Purpose: How to Create Healthy Communities* (Steve Gladen), Rick Warren, pastor of Saddleback Church, explains that he tells new members of his church that they will not feel truly connected to the faith community until they join and participate in a small faith group. He credits the success of his megachurch to the emphasis on small faith groups and believes that there are more people participating in church-sponsored small groups during the week than are attending Sunday worship, which averages over 20,000. If we are going to be a church on the move, we have to offer opportunities for people to develop personal relationships—including relationship with Christ—through small faith-sharing group experiences.

The church must grow larger and smaller at the same time—larger through worship (weekend services) and smaller through fellowship (small groups).
—Rick Warren, Pastor of Saddleback Church

Questions for Reflection and Discussion

- What groups do I belong to (not just church groups)? Why do I join groups?
- When have I felt most "at home" in a parish? Who was responsible for that?
- What experiences have I had with sharing faith in a small group?
- What does it mean that a church must grow larger and smaller at the same time?

40

From Saying Prayers to Praying Always

The Lord tells us: "the first task in life is this: prayer." But not the prayer of words, like a parrot; but the prayer, the heart: gazing on the Lord, hearing the Lord, asking the Lord.
—Pope Francis, daily homily, October 8, 2013

When two people get married, they exchange vows, words that express their love and commitment to one another. Many couples put a great deal of thought into wording their vows. I know that my wife, Joanne, and I worked at composing our own vows for our wedding day so that those words would capture and express our deepest thoughts, wishes, desires, and promises to each other. Now imagine what would have happened if, since that wonderful day in 1982 (you can do the math), I spent very little time with Joanne and rarely, if ever, shared any thoughts, hopes, dreams, fears, desires, sorrows, or joys with her. Instead, once in a while, if I remembered to do so, I perfunctorily recited out loud the words I composed for our wedding day, whether she was in the room or not. I have a feeling that I would not be wearing a wedding ring on my finger right now. That's not how relationships work.

When you love someone, you desire to spend time with that person. You long to feel close to him or her, and you desire to share intimate thoughts and feelings. You long to be close, even if words aren't being spoken—it's just good to be in this person's presence.

When it comes to our relationship with God—Father, Son, and Holy Spirit—I fear that too many of us are doing almost exactly what I just described above, as absurd as that scenario sounds. For too many Catholics, prayer can be reduced to reciting a few words—beautiful words, mind you—by memory each day and then patting ourselves on the back for fulfilling our obligation to pay at least some scant attention to the most important relationship in our lives. That's not a recipe for a healthy relationship. The result is that we find ourselves living in spiritual divorce, separated from our beloved.

If we are going to be a church on the move, we need to teach people what prayer is and how to pray. Many of us Catholics were taught to "say our prayers" as children, and thank goodness for that. But then something amazing happened. We grew up. And as we did so, we outgrew many things: our beds, our shoes, our clothes, and many of our habits. We also outgrew the way we prayed. For most of us, however, we were never taught how to pray as grown-ups. And so we approach prayer in one of the three following childish ways:

- like a child sitting on Santa's lap, asking him for what we want and promising to be good;
- like E.T., the Extra Terrestrial, thinking that we are separated from God but that if we pray hard enough and in just the right way ("E.T. phone home!"), God will respond and come to our rescue;
- like a child reciting a memorized poem or speech in front of our parents at an assembly, hoping for their approval of our efforts.

We need to teach adults how to pray like adults. So much of our adult faith formation goes into teaching the first three pillars of the *Catechism of the Catholic Church*: the creed (doctrine), the sacraments, and morality. We seem to forget that the fourth pillar is prayer. Prayer is a necessity, not frosting on the cake. Without a vibrant prayer life, we are not nurturing a relationship with God but simply staking membership in an organization that is loosely affiliated with him.

I propose that every parish look at its faith-formation program and identify whether and how people, especially adults, are being taught to pray. And this doesn't just mean that we should put the recitation of the rosary on the weekly parish calendar and hope that people show up. I'm talking about inviting people at every turn to engage in deeper, more meaningful experiences of prayer. For example:

- When people come to register as parishioners or for religious education or Catholic school, pray with them and gently invite them to mention who or what they want to pray for at that moment.

- When couples come for marriage preparation or baptismal preparation, lead them in a brief guided reflection, inviting them to visualize married life together and/or life with their newborn child and to share, silently or out loud, their deepest desires and hopes with God.

- When groups gather for parish meetings, make a habit of inviting people to share intercessions so that they become more accustomed to spontaneous prayer.

- When the parish gathers for Mass, invite those in the assembly (who wish to), to say out loud the names of those who are sick as well as the names of those who have died; if the assembly is not that large, invite any who wish to share personal petitions out loud.

- Offer workshops, classes, seminars, whatever you want to call them, in which people are invited to learn and practice adult ways to pray, such as meditation or the daily *examen*.
- Match parishioners up with prayer partners who commit to praying for one another during a liturgical season such as Advent or Lent.
- To assist parishioners in prayer, connect them with online resources such as the 3-Minute Retreat from Loyola Press or Sacred Space from the Irish Jesuits.

While there are many fine devotionals available to assist Catholics in their prayer lives, we also need to do more to teach adults how to pray in a way that, according to St. Ignatius, resembles one friend speaking to another. Unless we can help people pray as grown-ups and discover a life-giving relationship with the Lord, we have as much chance of becoming a church on the move as we do teaching pigs to fly.

———————

You don't know how to pray? Put yourself in the presence of God, and as soon as you have said, "Lord, I don't know how to pray!" you can be sure you've already begun.
—St. Josemaria Escriva

Questions for Reflection and Discussion

- Who taught me how to pray? How old was I? What did that prayer look and sound like?
- Have I been taught to pray as a grown-up? What is different about my prayer now, in my adulthood, than in my childhood?
- What obstacles do I still face in my personal prayer life?
- When am I most comfortable praying? With whom?

41

From Hearing with Our Ears to Listening with Our Hearts

Open up your heart and listen to what God is saying to you.
—Pope Francis, morning Mass, Casa Santa Marta, July 10, 2013

When I was a student at St. Ignatius College Prep back in the 1970s, I participated in a pilot program of spiritual direction, meeting every few weeks during my lunch break with Fr. Terry Baum, SJ, then a Jesuit scholastic. I recall how he encouraged me to listen for the voice of God in my prayer, which I did, patiently waiting and expecting that I would hear a voice say, "Hello, Joe, this is God. Here's what I want you to do." Alas, there were no voices. I went back to Fr. Terry and told him I wanted to quit the program because I wasn't hearing anything and concluded that I must be doing something wrong. It was then that Fr. Terry realized my problem: I was trying to listen with my ears. He explained that listening for God's voice is not something we do with our ears but with our heart. Since then, I've been trying to exercise this little-understood muscle.

I firmly believe that the concern I had as a high-school student continues to be a common concern for many Catholics, young and old. I don't think most of us have been taught how to listen for God's voice with our hearts. If we are going to be a church on the move, we need to help people develop this inner ear, the ability to hear God speaking not so much with words but with a voice that only our hearts can perceive.

While it would be nice to simply hear some words come forth from God's mouth right into our ears, at the same time, we are skeptical of people who claim that they hear God speak to them directly. For most of us, that's just not how it happens. God is much more subtle than that, which is exactly the point of the story in 1 Kings 19, in which Elijah encounters God, not in an earthquake, not in a fire, but in a gentle whisper. Here is a brief overview of just some of the ways God speaks to us subtly, beyond words, ways we often overlook and need to pay more attention to.

- **Thoughts.** In response to our prayer, God may be inviting us to pay closer attention to a thought that continues to rattle around inside our head, perhaps for no obvious reason.

- **Memories.** It is not unusual for God to stir up memories from our past in order to speak to us about something going on in the present.

- **Feelings.** Prayer does not always result in a good feeling; however, it is important to pay attention to any feelings that stir up within us when we are speaking with God. God may give you a feeling of peace and contentment to remind you of his presence, or perhaps a feeling of restlessness to stir you to action.

- **Hopes and desires.** At times, God speaks to us by stirring up hopes and desires within us. We may simply find ourselves more aware of a particular yearning. When people say that they are "going with their gut feeling," they often mean that they are following an inner hope or desire.

- **Dreams.** God has not given up on the notion of speaking to people in dreams. In *Dreams: God's Forgotten Language*, author John Sanford encourages us to pay attention to these images that come from within our unconscious self and to look for clues as to what God might be saying to us. It's important to know that dreams are not meant to be taken as literal messages from God but are vehicles for getting in touch with God's movement deep within us through symbols, concepts, or deep emotions.

- **Nature.** At times Catholics are suspicious of this notion of hearing God speak to us through nature because we fear entering the realm of New Age spirituality or the ancient, yet always prevalent, heresy of pantheism. Catholics do not equate nature with God, but we certainly believe that nature possesses God's fingerprints and that it reflects his presence, goodness, strength, power, and beauty.

- **Experiences.** God's message for us may be wrapped in an experience we have just been part of. Reflecting on our experiences is an important way of recognizing what God may be saying to us or asking of us.

- **Encounters with others.** Throughout Scripture, God used people as his mouthpieces, and he continues to do so. Each day, God speaks to us through other people's words and actions. By paying closer attention to the people we live with, work with, work for, serve, or just play with, we may discover God speaking to us.

- **Encounters with beauty.** Beyond nature, God speaks to us through any experience in which we encounter beauty. This includes music, drama, literature, athleticism, art, and more. Beauty provokes feelings within us, and very often those feelings are part of a wordless conversation with God. In fact, I propose that a good way for parishes to begin teaching this notion of listening to God with our hearts is to host a sacred art fair or to invite people to an experience of creating sacred art.

If some of this seems too esoteric for you, just picture yourself sitting on a porch swing with someone you love. You don't necessarily have to be speaking words with that person in order to feel as though you are making a connection with him or her. You can just sit there quietly, swaying back and forth in a gentle manner, perhaps holding hands, and experience intimacy without saying a word. In the same way, our connection with God often takes place beyond words. The subtlety of this conversation does, however, require that we practice discernment so that we can ascertain whether a message is coming from God, from our self, or even from a voice we should not be listening to. For further reading on this topic, I highly recommend *God's Voice Within: The Ignatian Way to Discover God's Will* by Mark Thibodeaux. By helping folks tune in to God's voice and to adjust the frequency so as to make a connection to a language beyond words, we can help the people of God become a vibrant and discerning church on the move.

―――――――――

The more spiritual a man is, the more he discontinues trying to make particular acts with his faculties, for he becomes more engrossed in one general, pure act, a calm and repose of interior quietude.
―St. John of the Cross

Questions for Reflection and Discussion

- How does God speak to me beyond words?
- Of the ways God speaks to us described above, which have I paid attention to? Which have I been ignoring?
- When might God have been speaking to me through a thought, memory, or feeling?
- When has God spoken to me through an experience or through another person?

42

From Strangely Schizophrenic
to Well-Balanced

Piety is not mere outward religiosity; it is that genuine religious spirit which makes us turn to the Father as his children and to grow in our love for others, seeing them as our brothers and sisters, members of God's family.
—Pope Francis, General Audience, June 4, 2014

First of all, I'd like to acknowledge that schizophrenia is a serious disorder that brings no small amount of suffering to those who have it and to those who love and care for them. I am using the word here in its secondary, less clinical definition to describe a characteristic found in the church that can be described as a "contrary or antagonistic quality or attitude" (Merriam-Webster). This tendency can be found on many levels, especially when it comes to politically charged issues and we find people aligning themselves (or labeling others) in either conservative or liberal camps. We're not even going to go there. If I can find a solution to that quagmire, it'll require more than a chapter (and the royalties I earn on that book will enable me to retire).

Instead, I'd like to talk about the schizophrenic tendencies we find in our parishes when it comes to the types of activities we offer for our parishioners. These activities seem to fall into two very disparate categories. On the one hand, we find activities that are unabashedly spiritual in nature. Here are examples from various parish bulletins.

- First Friday Eucharistic adoration
- Rosary group
- St. Peregrine Novena
- Baptismal Preparation
- Divine Mercy Chaplet
- Pilgrimage to Shrine of Christ's Passion

These activities are all fine and good, and the contrast I'm about to set up is not between good/bad, right/wrong, or anything along those lines. The following activities are also fine and good but are unabashedly secular in nature, usually designed to provide opportunities for parish folks to have fun with one another or to attract people to the parish community. Here are some common examples from various parish bulletins.

- Men's Club Final Four Party
- Women's Club Fashion Show
- A Day at the Racetrack
- Dinner and Candlelight Theater
- Smoker/Poker Party
- Parish Picnic

Again, I'm not promoting one list over the other. What I am pointing out, however, is that we can't ever seem to find a middle ground. We offer experiences that are either completely "churchy" in nature or completely secular in nature. We are not helping people find God in all things, which is at the heart of the Christian faith. If we are going to become a church on the move, we need to invite people to participate in a variety of everyday experiences and help them find

God in these experiences. In other words, we need to bring these two poles together and invite people to experience the sacred in the secular.

What would this look like? It is based not on trying to get people interested in something but on looking at what people are already doing and interested in and seeing how to bring a Catholic perspective to it. Here are some examples.

- **Theater and Theology:** an experience of theater (for example, *Les Miserables*) followed by discussion and presentation of Catholic values exemplified in the story
- **Volleyball and Values for Young Adults:** an opportunity for young adults to enjoy an evening of fun playing volleyball with a break in the middle to explore Catholic values
- **Balance Class: Mind, Body, and Soul:** a fitness class with a trained instructor that includes prayer, meditation, and spiritual reading
- **Running with the Rosary:** a running club that introduces participants to the use of a finger Rosary
- **Camping with Christ:** overnight camping that includes prayer experiences focused on the Liturgy of the Hours and Lectio Divina
- **Hiking toward Holiness:** an experience of hiking in which participants reflect on creation spirituality
- **Fishing for Faith:** an experience of fishing that invites participants to spend time in quiet meditation and develop the art of contemplation
- **Helping Hands Woodworking:** an invitation for woodworkers to create items to be given as gifts to those experiencing grief
- **Gardening with God:** an opportunity for folks with a green thumb to come together to get in touch with the rhythms of

planting seeds, growing, and harvesting and to be more in touch with God's creation

- **Finding God in Photography:** an opportunity for those interested in photography to pursue St. Ignatius's quest to find God in all things (see Picturing God, ignatianspirituality.com)

OK, I have a penchant for using alliteration, but that's just to show you that catchy labels can be dreamed up for these types of activities to make them more inviting and to show the connection to spirituality. Think of this as a twist on doing small faith-sharing groups (see chapter 39). There's no rule that such groups need to sit in a circle in someone's living room with a book or Bible in hand to be spiritual or catechetical. For many people, activities such as the ones above can provide a connection between their Catholic faith and some hobby or activity they have interest in. This approach can be a wonderful form of pre-evangelization, a way of inviting people to begin getting a flavor of the Catholic way of life without being overwhelmed by anything that smacks of being "churchy" too early on. Finally, activities such as these call for a whole new breed of catechists. No one can expect the pastor and staff to run all the above activities! Instead, it's an opportunity for parishes to recruit parishioners who have interests in these areas and work with them to form them in faith so that they, in turn, can connect others with the Catholic faith through these activities.

I sought to hear the voice of God and climbed the topmost steeple, but God declared: "Go down again—I dwell among the people."
—Blessed John Henry Newman

Questions for Reflection and Discussion

- Judging from my own parish's weekly bulletin or Web site, which activities seem to be strictly spiritual? Which seem to be strictly secular?
- In which strictly spiritual activity do I participate at my parish?
- In which mostly secular activity do I participate at my parish?
- What activities or hobbies are popular among people in my community that could make for potentially spiritual parish activities?

Part Five

How a Church on the Move Engages the World

43

From Country Club to Advocate for the Poor

We have to state, without mincing words, that there is an
inseparable bond between our faith and the poor. May we never
abandon them.
—Pope Francis, *Evangelii Gaudium*, 48

This chapter's brevity is not a mistake, nor is it the result of my being lazy and just wanting to finish this book. It is to make a point. In the Gospels, as far as social issues go, there was only one issue that Jesus returned to over and over again: the needs of the poor. In fact, Jesus refers to the needs of the poor three times more often than he refers to issues related to marriage and divorce. And yet, when the church engages the world, it often speaks the most and the loudest on issues related to sexual morality.

If we are going to be a church on the move, we need to be, first and foremost, about tending to the needs of those who are poor. Most of the giving that is asked for in parishes is targeted for parish expenses. Those expenses need to be covered. But how are we inviting the parish as a whole to serve the needs of those truly in need on a regular basis?

I propose that every parish make caring for those in need its number one priority—meaning, the social issue that is spoken about the most and responded to the most. Back in the 1990s, the late Bishop Kenneth E. Untener mandated that every meeting that took place in the Diocese of Saginaw over a three-month period start with this agenda item: "How will what we are doing here affect or involve people living in poverty?" Parishes such as Christ Our King Catholic Church in Mount Pleasant, South Carolina, indicate on their Web site each week that the first ten percent of the weekly collection is distributed to charitable organizations and needs. That's what I call making service to the poor a priority.

When someone steals another's clothes, we call them a thief. Should we not give the same name to one who could clothe the naked and does not? The bread in your cupboard belongs to the hungry; the coat unused in your closet belongs to the one who needs it; the shoes rotting in your closet belong to the one who has no shoes; the money which you hoard up belongs to the poor.
—St. Basil the Great

Questions for Reflection and Discussion

- What is my parish doing on a regular basis to serve the needs of those struggling in poverty?
- What am I personally doing on a regular basis to serve the needs of those who are in need?
- What would my parish need to do to make serving the poor its number-one priority?

44

From Single-Issue to Consistent Ethic

---

*We cannot insist only on issues related to abortion, gay marriage
and the use of contraceptive methods. . . . We have to find a
new balance; otherwise even the moral edifice of the church is
likely to fall like a house of cards.*
—Pope Francis, interview with Italian Jesuit journal
La Civiltà Cattolica, September, 2013

Imagine the following far-fetched yet illustrative scenario: there are
two candidates vying for election to the presidency of the United
States. The country is facing calamitous crises on both the domestic
and foreign fronts. Candidate A puts forth a detailed and doable
plan to address and correct the crises, but he or she is also
pro-choice. Candidate B is pro-life, but his or her only proposal
to address the numerous crises facing the country and the world is
to encourage everyone to wear smiley-face buttons. As a Catholic,
whom do you vote for? For some, the choice is easy: because abortion is an intrinsic evil, candidate B is the only choice. For many
Catholics, however, the choice is not that simple. While recognizing
the intrinsic evil of abortion, many Catholics may judge candidate
B as incapable of actually effecting change related to abortion as well
as to the other critical issues facing the country. At the same time,

despite candidate A's pro-choice stance, they may see him or her as best equipped for responding to the other crises at hand.

In other words, today's Catholics refuse to be relegated to a simplistic single-issue approach to engaging a very complex world. The world is simply not that black and white. Recognizing this, the late Joseph Cardinal Bernardin promoted a "consistent ethic of life" approach to moral issues, which sought to present church teaching as a unity (a "seamless garment") or a continuum on which life is protected and defended at every juncture. Bernardin insisted that this consistent ethic of life does not create an equivalence between the taking of innocent human life (abortion) and the promotion of life (health care, economic issues, housing) but rather insists on an interrelatedness between them. In fact, Cardinal Bernardin's specific goal was to bridge the chasm between conservatives and liberals by getting them to see the interconnectedness of the issues they each championed: pro-life on the right and social justice on the left.

Unfortunately, both sides of the political spectrum have dug in their heels, and the polarization has only gotten worse. Some liberal politicians created a parody of Cardinal Bernardin's consistent ethic to justify their other social-justice efforts while remaining mum on the taking of innocent life through abortion. Sadly, some conservatives, instead of rallying to correct this parody of the seamless garment approach, chose instead to accept the parody as the real thing and to condemn the consistent-ethic approach. And just as some liberals have "taken cover" behind the parody of the seamless garment approach to justify their support of abortion on demand, some conservatives have "taken cover" behind their own parody of the principle of "prudential judgment," resulting in an unwavering condemnation of abortion while seemingly settling for what author Jerry Bridges calls "respectable sins"—support for policies that ignore the sanctity of human life outside of the womb (*Respectable Sins:*

Confronting the Sins We Tolerate). Hiding behind the notion of "prudential judgment" is precisely the kind of sin of omission that Jesus warned about in the Parable of the Rich Man and Lazarus (Luke 16:19–31). Such an approach, for example, has led to the distasteful fact that support for torture of terrorist suspects—something the church condemns as an intrinsic evil (*Catechism* 2297–98)—is significantly higher among self-identified "pro-life" Catholics (and evangelicals) than those who profess no religion at all (*Washington Post*-ABC News Poll, December 11, 2014).

Well, Pope Francis has had enough of both these erroneous ends of the spectrum.

The Holy Father's insistence on a "new balance" in our rhetoric is his way of calling for a "consistent ethic of life" so that we are not seen as a single-issue church. He said as much when he addressed the U.S. Congress in 2015 and called on its members to "defend life at every stage of development." And his call is resonating with Catholics and non-Catholics alike, especially with young people who care deeply about issues related to the environment, the economy, and social justice, as well as about the protection of the unborn. He is not suggesting a moral equivalence with regard to these issues but an interrelatedness. Pope Francis recognizes that just as World War II was won on both the Western and Eastern fronts, the battles we are fighting as a church are taking place on many fronts, but they are against a common enemy that is defeated by the one weapon we carry: mercy.

On the parish level, the way forward is mapped out for us nicely by Franciscan Fr. Richard Rohr, who reminds us that discipleship is not primarily about being *correct* but is much more about being *connected*. At present, we are tending to operate as though discipleship can be reduced to taking the "correct" stance on hot-button issues.

The key, instead, is for us as a church (and as a parish) to ask how we are *connected* to

- the unborn,
- unwed mothers with unwanted pregnancies,
- those who are gay,
- victims of gun violence and domestic abuse,
- our environment,
- those without employment,
- those without homes,
- those without healthcare,
- victims of racism,
- those who are divorced, and
- those who are sick and dying.

We are not called simply to have a correct stance on these issues. We are called to have a womb-to-tomb connection to those whose lives and dignity are at risk. And that connection must be manifested in action and works of mercy, not just in the voting booth. To accomplish this, I recommend that parishes begin every announcement related to human concerns with the following words: "Because we are dedicated to protecting the dignity of human life from the womb to the tomb, our parish will be . . . [name and describe whatever action is taking place]."

In this way, the message will be made clear and consistent: all our efforts to protect the dignity of human life are interrelated, and they begin with protecting the unborn.

In order for us to be a church on the move, we can no longer be squabbling with one another over who is more correct. The results of that have been paralyzing. St. Ignatius insisted that discipleship invites us to hold profound reverence for each person as he or she is. To do this, we need to focus on how we are connecting with those whose lives and dignity are threatened, from the womb to the tomb. Armed with mercy, we can mobilize on numerous fronts, combatting a common enemy: those forces that drive people to despair.

———————

Society as a whole must respect, defend and promote the dignity of every human person, at every moment and in every condition of that person's life.
—Pope John Paul II, *Evangelium Vitae*, 81

Questions for Reflection and Discussion

- What would inform my decision in the scenario (candidate A and candidate B) proposed at the outset of the chapter?
- How can a consistent ethic of life bridge the chasm between conservatives and liberals?
- What does it mean to say that discipleship is less about being correct and more about being connected?
- What effect could it have on my parish if every human-concerns announcement was prefaced with "Because we are dedicated to protecting the dignity of human life from the womb to the tomb . . ."?

45

From Going My Way
to Going Green

If the simple fact of being human moves people to care for the environment of which they are a part, Christians in their turn "realize that their responsibility within creation, and their duty towards nature and the Creator, are an essential part of their faith."
—Pope Francis, *Laudato Si,* 64

There is no shortage of Hollywood movies with apocalyptic or post-apocalyptic themes. Most of these films have one thing in common: there are typically a few humans who survive whatever apocalyptic tragedy has taken place. One movie, however, took quite a different approach: Pixar's *Wall-E* (2008). The film takes place 700 years in the future and portrays earth as completely uninhabited. There is no "last man standing." In fact, the first half hour of the film has no dialogue. Instead, we watch as a garbage-collecting robot named Wall-E scurries about, futilely attempting to clean up the planet, which is buried in filth and waste; the earth itself is the victim of humankind's blatant disregard for the well-being of the planet. On the surface, the movie can be mistaken for a remake of *Finding Nemo,* with a robot instead of a fish—just a cute children's movie. In reality, however, the movie stands as a sobering indictment of our blatant disregard for the environment.

All around us, our beautiful planet Earth is showing signs of decay and death because of the carelessness of humanity. Meanwhile, we go along seemingly oblivious to the destruction that is occurring and the danger that lurks ahead for future generations. I am grateful that in Pope Francis we have a leader in our church who has raised his voice to announce that caring for the environment is a matter of faith. In his encyclical *Laudato Si: On Care for Our Common Home*, Pope Francis issued a clarion call to respond to the cries of our suffering planet.

If we are going to become a church on the move, we must embrace the pope's call to care for our common home, shed the laid-back image of the church portrayed in the 1944 film *Going My Way*, and instead commit to an aggressive campaign of "going green." When an atheist such as comedian Bill Maher—someone who loathes religion and despises the Catholic Church—praises Pope Francis for issuing an encyclical dealing with climate change, it's pretty safe to say that the pope's message is moving people, something that a church on the move needs to do. Caring for the planet is an issue of great importance to young people, who increasingly view institutional religion as irrelevant and out of touch with important issues. In an article for *America* magazine (June 18, 2015), author and speaker Kerry Weber lays out an argument for why *Laudato Si* is the perfect encyclical for millennials, primarily because the issue of climate change remains one of this generation's top concerns. Weber points out that the Holy Father himself sees this as a crucial issue for reaching out to young adults when he says, "Young people demand change. They wonder how anyone can claim to be building a better future without thinking of the environmental crisis and the sufferings of the excluded" (*Laudato Si*, 13).

So, having said all the above, what can parishes do to promote care for the environment aside from encouraging people, especially millennials, to read *Laudato Si*? They can follow the lead of Archbishop Blase Cupich, who announced in 2015 that the Chicago Archdiocese would be the first in the nation to commit to tracking water and energy use and pollution emissions by investing in energy-saving initiatives at every one of its 2,700-plus buildings. Following this example, parishes might pursue the following:

- Establish a parish "creation-care group" to oversee all parish efforts to protect the environment and focus efforts on recruiting young adults to serve in this capacity.
- Place recycling receptacles in all parish gathering areas.
- Initiate an annual or ongoing beautification effort, with an emphasis on planting trees, not only on parish grounds but throughout the parish community.
- Encourage a parish car-pool ministry that invites people to cut down on the number of cars needed to bring people to Mass and other parish functions.
- Encourage a variety of encounters with nature—outdoor activities such as hiking and camping—that include time for prayer and meditation.
- Conduct a "green" audit of the parish facilities, looking at water-use efficiency and energy-use efficiency.
- For smaller parish gatherings, replace disposable cups, plates, and utensils with reusable items.
- Have some "green" liturgies, perhaps tied to Earth Day or the Feast of St. Francis of Assisi.
- Create a "*Laudato Si*/Go Green" bulletin board/table in a public space on parish grounds or establish a link on the parish Web site.

- Create reusable shopping bags with the parish logo on them and sell them, with all profits going to "go green" activities in the parish.
- Devise strategies for households in the parish to participate in protecting the environment; bring in an expert to talk about composting, growing vegetables in pots or small gardens, using rain barrels, or winterizing homes for greater energy efficiency.

Pope Francis's call to protect our planet is not some call to political correctness. Rather, it is a call to deepen our relationship with God and one another by focusing on the great gift of creation God has given us to share with one another. In his *Jesuit Post* article, "An Overview of Laudato Si," (June 18, 2015), Henry Longbottom, SJ, explains that the Holy Father's encyclical is all about relationships—our familial relationship with our planet and our relationship with other humans, both of which we are damaging. He states that "[w]e are forgetting our interconnectedness with the earth and with those around and ahead of us who depend on our good stewardship of the gift of creation." A church on the move is one that recognizes and respects this interconnectedness and is mobilizing to do something about it.

To commit a crime against the natural world is a sin. . . . For humans . . . to destroy the biological diversity of God's creation; for humans to degrade the integrity of Earth by causing changes in its climate, by stripping the earth of its natural forests or destroying its wetlands; . . . For human beings to contaminate the Earth's waters, its land, its air, and its life . . . these are sins.
—Patriarch Bartholomew, Address in Santa Barbara, November 8, 1997

Questions for Reflection and Discussion

- How is the call to protect the planet we live on connected to our call to love one another?
- How is protecting the environment connected to our life of faith?
- What am I doing to be more environmentally friendly? What else could I be doing?
- What is my parish doing to be more environmentally friendly? What else could and should my parish be doing?

46

From Fulfilling Obligations to Living Heroically

Following and accompanying Christ, staying with him,
demands "coming out of ourselves," requires us to be outgoing; to
come out of ourselves, out of a dreary way of living faith that
has become a habit, out of the temptation to withdraw into our
own plans which end by shutting out God's creative action.
—Pope Francis, General Audience, March 27, 2013

Fear can be a great motivator. When I was growing up, religion classes at St. Casimir Elementary School in Chicago regularly included filmstrips (the great cutting-edge technology of the 1960s) that always seemed to include depictions of people burning in hell. For many of us growing up at that time, the primary reason for going to church was to avoid the fires of hell, which would consume us if we did not go. While we Catholics still hold that intentionally skipping Mass for no good reason does serious harm to our relationship with God and others, people today (especially millennials) insist on being given a better reason for waking up on Sunday than fear of hell. That's not to say that millennials don't respect the notion of obligation. It simply means that they want to know *why* something is an obligation. And the response has to be something better than,

"Because if you don't, you'll go to hell." Many people today simply don't see going to church as an obligation that is worth the time and effort.

If we are going to become a church on the move, we need to move beyond satisfying obligation and invite people to live heroically. Young people, especially, are attracted to involvement in something that they clearly perceive as a movement. The job of the church is to help them recognize discipleship as entering a heroic movement—God's movement. We need to "market" the church, not as a safe oasis where people dream of floating on clouds for all eternity (which, by the way, is a horrible image of heaven!) but as an edgy place where folks grapple with hard truths that compel them to participate in activities that might even carry a hint of risk or danger.

This is, no doubt, why countless numbers of people, especially young adults, flock to participate each year in an annual three-day, sixty-mile walk to help end breast cancer. No one is under obligation to do this demanding task. And yet folks eagerly respond to promotional ads that are filled with inspiring stories of people making a heroic commitment to participate in this grueling event in support of a noble cause. Perhaps, each Lent, if we presented fasting and abstaining as heroic actions rather than obligations or regulations to fulfill, we might inspire more people to not only observe but also embrace these disciplines.

What exactly does it mean to live heroically? In *Beyond Success: The 15 Secrets to Effective Leadership and Life*, Brian D. Biro explains that one thing all real heroes have in common is that they use every fiber of their being to do something that makes a profoundly positive difference in the lives of others. We will not become a church on the move by simply asking people to fulfill obligations and to follow regulations. Rather, we need to discover ways to invite people to make a profound positive impact in the lives of others.

Heroic living is a characteristic of Ignatian spirituality. In his books *Heroic Leadership* and *Heroic Living*, Chris Lowney describes the concept of *magis* (Latin for "more") as the foundation of heroism. Lowney explains that Jesuits are taught to always seek to do "the more"—not simply adding on more activity but developing an attitude that is never content to just go through the motions and always seeks something greater. Pastoral leadership in our parishes needs to call people to this heroic spirit of *magis*: a dissatisfaction with the status quo and a restless desire for something greater. According to Lowney, this type of heroic leadership inspires heroic living, a way of life characterized by the desire to live according to a "mighty purpose." Pastoral leadership can create a culture of heroism by consistently inviting people to

- read the lives of the saints to cultivate virtues that can propel us on our own heroic path;
- work for gospel-inspired change and transformation in the world;
- discern what God is calling them to do (all great heroes have a "calling");
- participate in positive efforts to do good rather than just oppose evil (Blessed Mother Teresa famously said that she would not participate in an antiwar rally but would definitely participate in a pro-peace rally);
- imaginatively and discerningly peruse the many opportunities the parish provides to find the right situation that will enable them to act heroically;
- never overlook the heroism of simple acts of kindness (your simple gesture of kindness may very well be the miracle someone was praying for).

Heroes do not have to wear capes or possess superpowers. We all have heroes in our own lives, those people who on one or more occasions used every fiber of their being to make a profound difference in our life. The call to follow Christ is nothing less than heroic. Discipleship is about much more than being nice to others. It is about laying down our lives for others, which does not necessarily mean to physically die but to set aside our own needs in favor of tending to the needs of others. Parents and spouses do this every day. In fact, anyone who unselfishly and sincerely provides a service to another person, even when receiving remuneration, is heroically laying down his or her life for others: teachers, first responders, customer-service representatives, medical personnel, hairdressers, flight attendants, and so on. To make this more obvious to people, I propose that parish bulletins regularly include profiles of heroes: members of the parish who are heroically laying their lives down for others. No matter what situation they find themselves in, heroes make a habit of having the best interests of others in mind. And I can think of no purpose mightier than participating in God's plan of salvation.

There is in me a longing to be real, to be authentic, to be a clear reflection of what my heart holds at its deepest levels. It is a goal that the gospel steadfastly holds up as an invitation to me, to the church. It is when the church embraces the gospel selflessly that it bears the heart of God and becomes real to the world. And when it is real, the church makes God believable.
—Gary Smith, SJ, *Radical Compassion: Finding Christ in the Heart of the Poor*

Questions for Reflection and Discussion

- Who is a personal hero for me? How did this person make a profound difference in my life?
- Which saint inspires me as being truly heroic? Why?
- What does it mean to have a "mighty purpose" in life?
- What are some of the ways I lay down my life for others (set aside my own needs to tend to the best interests of others) each day?

47

From Talking at the World to Interacting with the World

In [Jesus] was revealed the grace, the mercy, and the tender love of the Father: Jesus is Love incarnate. He is not simply a teacher of wisdom, he is not an ideal for which we strive while knowing that we are hopelessly distant from it. He is the meaning of life and history, who has pitched his tent in our midst.
—Pope Francis, homily at Vigil Mass for Christmas, December 24, 2013

Perhaps one of the most well-known (and certainly one of my favorite) Ignatian principles is the concept of trying to persuade people by "entering through their door but being sure to leave through your door." In essence, St. Ignatius was speaking about the concept of inculturation long before that term was invented. Even now, the notion of inculturation is greatly misunderstood by many who settle for a narrow definition that sees it as the inclusion of various ethnic groups in worship style and overall parish life. This doesn't even come close to the true meaning of inculturation, which is to enter into—to immerse oneself—in the overall experience of another individual or group and to proclaim the word of God from within that reality. It is much easier, unfortunately, to lob verbal grenades from a distance in hopes that we will shake things up. For too long and with too many groups perceived as "outside" the usual parameters of the church, we have been lobbing grenades—talking at the world instead of engaging it and proclaiming the word of God from within that reality. We much prefer to stand on the safety of our own shores and shout at people across the ponds that separate us, hoping that they will either swim across to join us or stay far away from us.

The Incarnation is the ultimate example of inculturation. God did not settle for sending messages to humanity from up above, hoping that we might repent. Rather, he became one of us. He "pitched his tent" among us. He entered through our door and revealed his Word from within our reality. Another powerful example of this is Jesus entering the waters of the Jordan to be baptized. He did not need to do this, and John the Baptist said as much when he objected, "I need to be baptized by you, and do you come to me?" (Matthew 3:14). Jesus' response, "Let it be so now," shows Jesus' willingness to enter the murky waters of the Jordan, waters polluted not just with human filth but with sin that had been washed away by baptismal rituals. Jesus was not afraid of getting dirty.

If we are going to be a church on the move, we need to move from where we are to stand with those we serve and seek to engage. We need to look for their doors and enter into their reality and proclaim the Word of God from within that reality. What might that look like? Take, for example, the way we speak to adults and seek to form them. Our approach is not unlike the approach used in a child's game, Red Rover, in which a player on one side shouts to the other side, "Red Rover, Red Rover, let [name] come over!" We announce to people where we as a church stand, and we invite them to come over and join us. We are like a doctor who prescribes medicine for patients without necessarily doing a thorough examination, getting to know their history, or listening to them describe their symptoms.

True inculturation requires that we, first and foremost, enter people's lives and listen to them describe their needs. A good way to do this is to invite people to gather around life issues as opposed to gathering around doctrinal concepts. Here is a sampling of offerings that are focused on life issues.

- Celebrating life
- Getting through difficult times
- Letting go
- Coping with change
- Living heroically
- Finding your source of energy
- Developing deeper wisdom
- Discovering courage
- Reaching out to others
- Living a more meaningful life
- Coming to terms with suffering
- Becoming a more loving person
- Becoming a more selfless you
- Learning from failure

Another important strategy for a church is to host listening sessions. It's too easy to approach engagement with the world as a monologue rather than a dialogue. Parishes should regularly host listening sessions in which people know they are not going to be talked at but will be listened to in a nonjudgmental setting. St. Rita Catholic Community in Dallas, Texas, did this in 2015 when they invited parishioners "from teens on up" to attend a series of listening sessions so that the parish could be more in touch with what's going on in the lives of parishioners and how the church and the parish can be a part of that. Their stated hope was to build a community and to strengthen relationships. We tend to think of evangelization as telling others our story, when in reality it requires that we listen to others' stories. Listening sessions should be a way of life in Catholic parishes, not something that's offered only once in a while when leadership is changing or a capital campaign is being undertaken.

Dietrich Bonhoeffer once wrote, "Many people are looking for an ear that will listen. They do not find it among Christians, because Christians are talking when they should be listening." Ouch. Christians, entrusted by Jesus with the ministry of reconciliation, should be the best listeners in the world. After the synod on the New Evangelization in 2012, the bishops of the world encouraged the church to model our evangelization efforts after Jesus, who listened intently to the woman at the well who had come searching to fill her empty bucket. A church on the move needs to engage the world not only by speaking but also by listening so that we might help people fill their empty buckets, not with "polluted waters" but with living water.

———————

Inculturation . . . is not simply an external adaptation designed to make the Christian message more attractive or superficially decorative. On the contrary, it means the penetration of the deepest strata of persons and peoples by the Gospel which touches them deeply, "going to the very centre and roots" of their cultures.
—General Directory for Catechesis, 109

Questions for Reflection and Discussion

- When have I entered deeply into a culture different from my own? What do I remember about that experience?
- What does St. Ignatius mean when he says that when seeking to persuade others to our point of view, we need to "enter by their door but be sure to leave through your door?"
- What other examples would fit in the above list of a "needs-based" approach to faith formation?
- Why is listening an important part of evangelization?

48

From Debating to Storytelling

It always pains me greatly to discover how some Christian communities, and even consecrated persons, can tolerate different forms of enmity, division, calumny, defamation, vendetta, jealousy and the desire to impose certain ideas at all costs, even to persecutions which appear as veritable witch hunts. Whom are we going to evangelize if this is the way we act?
—Pope Francis, *Evangelii Gaudium*, 100

Here is a reply posted in the comments section of a blog:

"I wanted to suggest that you insert a needle into your skull and suck your own brain out. Upon reflection, however, I realized that would not be necessary as that seems to have been done previously" (as reported by Grant Gallicho, *dotCommonweal*, August 23, 2011).

Lovely, eh? Would it shock you to learn that this comment was made by a Catholic blogger speaking to another Catholic—an editor of a Catholic periodical—with whom he had a disagreement? That'll make folks line up to become Catholic, don't you think? Unfortunately, some of the most eye-popping examples of hateful vitriol on the Internet can be found on Catholic sites. This sad reality can be traced to our mistaken notion that we can debate people into discipleship as we strive to argue them into submission so that they have no choice but to recognize their own stupidity, then surrender and embrace the truth as we see it.

The truth is, we don't make disciples of Jesus Christ by engaging others in debate, especially not debate that is poisoned by hateful speech. And while it may be true that Jesus occasionally used harsh language when confronting the scribes and Pharisees, more often than not, his preferred method of engaging others and teaching about the kingdom was through storytelling—through parables. The parables of Jesus are the primary vehicle for conveying what Dr. Matthew Halbach, Catholic author and speaker, calls "the language and the logic of the kingdom of God" ("What Parables Can Teach the Synod Fathers and the Church Today," *Catechetical Leader*, March 2015). Halbach explains that parables invite listeners into a liminal space, a threshold between the world we see and the kingdom that is a reality that remains unseen unless its values are lived by its "inhabitants." Jesus used these deceptively simple stories to call people into new ways of thinking and living, to challenge listeners to "love outside the limits of one's own imagination, prejudices, and preferences" (Halbach).

If we are going to be a church on the move, we need to invite people to new ways of thinking and living, and we need to do so beyond polemics. An unfortunate by-product of the explosion of social media over the past several decades has been a comparable explosion in Catholic apologetics Web sites that tend to be arrogant in tone, argumentative, and triumphalistic. This approach reduces Catholicism to an intellectual debating society, lacking the beauty, depth, and warmth of the gospel of Jesus Christ as lovingly transmitted by the Catholic Church over two thousand years. People do not want to be lectured to about principles of dogma. However, they are more open to hearing a story about an everyday life experience in which God's nearness is revealed. If we are going to be a church on the move, we've got to learn to become storytellers rather than debaters.

To be better storytellers, however, each of us needs to become more aware of our own story. Many Catholics, baptized as infants and sacramentalized as little children, often come to the erroneous conclusion that they do not have a story to tell—no dramatic conversion that brought them as an adult to the waters of baptism and a whole new way of life. So how can we get in touch with our own story? Try the following:

- **Identify significant people in your life.** Just as God spoke to his people through Moses and the prophets, God typically speaks to us through other people. Who are the significant people in your life who have shaped and influenced you and to whom you owe much? No doubt once you think of these significant people, you will recall stories related to their impact on your life.

- **Identify moments of joy (big or small).** Throughout Scripture, people who recognize that they have had an encounter with God express that encounter in terms of great joy. By reversing that process, we can come to recognize encounters with God. In other words, by reflecting on moments of joy, whether big or small, we can recognize and tell stories about God's movement in our lives.

- **Identify peak moments of grace.** In addition to the everyday, small ways that God has manifested his presence to us, each of us can think of a handful of extraordinary moments when we felt we had come face-to-face with the infinite and when God's presence was almost palpable. Perhaps it was a brush with death, a moment of incredible luck or fortune, a dramatic recovery from an unfortunate situation, or an extraordinary experience of beauty. Moments like these make us aware of a power greater than our own and make for inspiring stories.

- **Identify milestones in your life.** Each of us can identify significant moments when we reach a milestone: a graduation, a new job, a promotion, a birthday or anniversary, a wedding day, and so on. These events cause us to pause and express gratitude, and when we express gratitude, we find ourselves contemplating the Giver of all good gifts. A story about a milestone in your life becomes a story of faith when you acknowledge God's grace present within the story.

I propose that parishes regularly feature stories of faith, told by everyday parishioners—in the parish bulletin, on parish bulletin boards, and on the parish Web site and Facebook page. The parish can recruit an individual or a small group of individuals to coordinate these efforts as they identify and invite parishioners to write short reflections (200 words) based on one of the above categories. Photos of the individuals who write their reflections can accompany their piece so that parishioners can begin to recognize others in their midst who are working at recognizing God in their everyday lives.

Storytelling creates an emotional connection that cannot be achieved through debate. If we are to become a church on the move, we need to touch not only people's minds but also their hearts.

People almost invariably arrive at their beliefs not on the basis of proof but on the basis of what they find attractive.
—Blaise Pascal, *The Art of Persuasion*

Questions for Reflection and Discussion

- What examples have I encountered of "Catholics behaving badly" on the Internet?
- Whom do I know who is a good storyteller? What makes an effective storyteller?
- Which of the four prompts above would I find easiest to respond to in order to identify a story of faith from my own life?
- What is one of my own stories of faith?

49

From Waiting for the Doorbell to Ring, to Ringing Doorbells

We cannot keep ourselves shut up in parishes, in our
communities, in our parish or diocesan institutions, when so
many people are waiting for the Gospel! To go out as ones sent.
It is not enough to simply open the door in welcome because they
come, but we must go out through that door to seek and meet
the people!
—Pope Francis, homily for the Mass with the Brazilian Bishops,
July 27, 2013

It was a dark and stormy evening in the spring of 1995, when my wife and I thought we heard our doorbell ring between thunder-claps. I went to open the front door to our new home in Evergreen Park, just a block outside of Chicago, and saw an elderly priest in a cassock walking away. I knew immediately that it was a priest I had heard stories about: Msgr. Francis McElligott, the legendary pastor emeritus of St. John Fisher Parish in whose boundaries we now resided. I called out, "Monsignor?" He quickly turned and said, "Ah, there you are," in his charming Irish brogue. "I just thought I'd stop by and welcome you to the parish." I invited him in for a lovely visit and a cup of coffee with my wife, my kids, and myself. After the storm died down a bit, he was on his way, but not before telling us that he'd see us at Mass on Sunday.

As it turns out, Msgr. McElligott had a huge map of the parish on the wall in his room, with pins in it to indicate new residents—information gleaned from local real-estate agents. This man knew what it meant to be a church on the move. Msgr. McElligott knew that it wasn't enough to sit back and wait for the doorbell to ring. Rather, he went out and rang doorbells, welcoming people to the parish and telling them that he looked forward to seeing them at Mass on Sunday!

Contrast Msgr. McElligott's philosophy and approach with another parish I once visited to drop off some resources on a bright, sunny weekday afternoon. I parked near what I thought looked like either the rectory or parish office and rang the bell. No answer. I rang and rang. No answer. I located several other doors to several other parish buildings and rang doorbells and knocked. No answer anywhere. Eventually, I gave up. There was not a single human being to be found anywhere on the church premises.

If we are going to be a church on the move, we need to follow the example of Msgr. McElligott and get out into our communities and ring doorbells instead of waiting for folks to show up at the parish office. In the spirit of Msgr. McElligott, I propose that every Catholic parish find two people (if you are seeking to persuade people, it helps to have someone to back you up!) to begin a door-to-door ministry. Catholics tend to be hesitant about the door-to-door approach, thinking that it smacks of proselytizing. It's high time we reconsidered. Certainly we don't want to engage in proselytizing; however, door-to-door ministry/outreach can be an effective way to let people know that the Catholic Church cares and welcomes. Such visits could offer an opportunity for a couple of parish representatives to provide some information about the parish, perhaps invite people to a specific event, ask if they have any needs that the parish can assist with, and ask if there is anyone or anything for whom/which they can pray. No debates about whether or not you're saved or how many years it's been since your last confession!

The notion of Catholics doing door-to-door ministry is not new: a number of dioceses have undertaken initiatives for this approach to evangelizing. Some of the practices they hold in common include the following:

- Pray before you start and between homes.
- Make sure only one person does the talking; you don't want to overwhelm.
- Don't sell anything.
- Invite, don't confront.
- Identify which parish you are from, and explain that your purpose is to welcome and invite.
- Be prepared to meet Catholics and non-Catholics alike.
- Affirm worshipping non-Catholics, and ask for mutual prayers for one another and for Christian unity.
- Ask them if they have any questions about the parish or the Catholic Church.
- Ask them if they have any urgent needs or prayer requests they would like to share with you.
- Leave some parish/Catholic literature.

If St. Ignatius could send his followers out to every corner of the world, how hard can it be for every Catholic parish to find two people to visit homes in the community? Does it take more than two? Most likely, but one of the reasons we are often hesitant to take on new ministries is because we make them out to be too large and overwhelming. If you want to start with more than two people, no one is stopping you! I'm just suggesting that two people who are willing to go door-to-door in the name of a Catholic parish can lay the foundation for making a huge difference in how that parish is perceived and in how that parish interacts with the community. Over time, such a ministry can grow and develop.

For those folks who are brave enough to visit our parish church before we've had a chance to invite them, we need to provide pew cards (guest cards/welcome cards) to welcome individuals and to invite them to indicate any needs or interests they may have. When I was in parish ministry, I invited a retired daily Mass attendee to walk through every pew in the church once a week to make sure that each one was supplied with pew cards and golf pencils. This simple task can also be assigned to several teens as a way to give them some responsibility behind the scenes. Church-supply companies offer pew welcome cards in quantities at a very low cost, or you can create and print your own. Whenever a pew card was received, a welcome packet was mailed out and a phone call followed. Not a few of the folks who filled out a welcome card became inquirers in the RCIA.

Whether we are going door-to-door or providing welcome cards or both, the bottom line is, if we are going to be a church on the move, we need to follow the example of Msgr. McElligott and be proactive in welcoming people and inviting them to join us.

———————

Many, many people hereabouts are not becoming Christians for one reason only: there is nobody to make them Christians.
—St. Francis Xavier

Questions for Reflection and Discussion

- What experiences—positive and negative—have I had of evangelizers ringing my doorbell? How can Catholic door-to-door ministry be uniquely Catholic and not a form of proselytizing?
- Why are Catholics generally hesitant about door-to-door ministry?
- To what parish events and activities could representatives from my parish invite people when they make door-to-door visits? What kind of information about my parish would be most important to share in such visits?
- How comfortable would I be doing door-to-door ministry?

50

From Maintenance to Mission and Mercy

Total openness to serving others is our hallmark; it alone is our title of honor! . . . We will not find the Lord unless we truly accept the marginalized. . . . Truly . . . the Gospel of the marginalized is where our credibility is at stake, is discovered and is revealed!

—Pope Francis, homily, February 15, 2015

When I was on the faculty of the high-school seminary in the Archdiocese of Chicago, we used to evaluate those students who applied to move on to the college seminary. Faculty members would speak to the strengths, weaknesses, involvements, and accomplishments of each candidate. Often there was heated debate, because faculty members saw different sides of the same student. Once, however, the complete opposite happened. A student's name came up, and the floor was open for comments. Silence ensued. It turned out that after four years in our school, this particular student had not made an impression on anyone, for better or for worse. He just stayed under the radar. Without any major objections, however, it became clear that there was nothing technically preventing his persevering on to the next step toward eventual ordination. It also became abundantly clear that we were dealing with a very flawed process for approving seminarians for the next step toward ordination: one that seemed to reward mediocrity. As long as you didn't stand out too much, you stood a good chance of getting all the way to ordination day.

Such a system creates "leaders" who are very good at maintaining the status quo and not stirring things up. They, in turn, lead parishes that are very good at maintaining the status quo. The system doesn't deal with us laypeople any more effectively. After working in the archdiocesan system for twenty years, I came to see that the system was more likely than not to reward mediocrity over creativity. Creative ideas cost money and stretched resources, human and otherwise. It was just easier for the system to reward those who didn't stir the pot too much. As a result, archdiocesan services tended to reward people who were good at maintaining the status quo. The end result is a church that is stuck in maintenance mode.

The problem with being in maintenance mode is that it prevents an organization from adapting to a rapidly changing world. While our core teachings remain unchanged, we as a church must learn how to adapt to the changes going on all around us if we are truly to become a church on the move. Our quest should never be simply survival or maintenance but rather growth. Always, growth! In *Autopsy of a Deceased Church: 12 Ways to Keep Yours Alive*, author Thom S. Rainer insists that too many churches follow paths that cause them to die and that churches in maintenance mode are experiencing a slow erosion toward that end. Sadly, the erosion that is slowly eating away at many of our parishes is occurring precisely because they are stuck in a maintenance model that is perfectly designed to produce just that result. And because the erosion is slow, folks have no sense of urgency—no sense of a need to change. Rainer emphasizes a common thread in all the churches on which he performed "autopsies": they had turned inward, focusing on their own needs, their own facilities, and their own preferences. He laments that for many churches, Jesus' Great Commission (Matthew 28:16–20, "Go, therefore . . .") has become instead the "Great Omission."

Paradoxically, the key to church growth is *not* to focus on growing the church; the Holy Spirit does that. The key to church growth is to focus on growing the church's presence in people's lives. Church growth happens when the church helps people grow, especially in their awareness of God's presence and activity in their daily lives. We need to focus not so much on how to get more people into the church but on how we, as church, can enter people's lives. The key to breaking out of maintenance mode is to turn our focus outward.

I propose that every parish commit to an annual major outreach project—symbolic of many other smaller projects—the focus of which is outward.

- Each year, the parish leadership would identify perhaps six to eight needs in the community as possible targets for outreach, while leaving the door open for parishioners to bring up other possibilities as well. Examples: senior housing, park beautification, homeless shelters, health care, local nonprofit social agencies in need of support.
- Parishioners would be invited to select the cause for the parish's outreach focus that year.
- The parish would pledge a certain amount of money as "seed money" to fuel the parish efforts.
- A steering committee would be formed to brainstorm ways that parishioners can participate in the outreach, either by raising additional money for the cause or by identifying other ways to provide support.

- Every year this outreach would be a point of pride for the parish and a way to invite people in the community to become part of a movement that is always focused outward.

One of the most best-known parables of Jesus is that of the Mustard Seed. Jesus compares the kingdom of God to this tiniest of seeds that grows into a large tree in which the birds can nest. What many of us don't realize is that the mustard plant is really a weed that, once it begins growing, is very hard to stop; it spreads and grows widely and quickly. It just keeps on reaching outward. Jesus is saying that this is the movement of the kingdom of God: outward—always outward. This outward movement is at the heart of a church on the move.

The greatest thing in this world is not so much where we stand as in what direction we are moving.
—attributed to Johann Wolfgang von Goethe

Questions for Reflection and Discussion

- What experience(s) have I had in a system that rewarded mediocrity?
- What causes organizations to get locked into maintenance mode?
- What causes organizations to develop an inward (insular) focus? How can that be changed?
- Looking at the activities in my own parish, can I identify how much energy is going outward and how much is moving inward? What can be done to shift focus outward?

51

From Regal to Humble

The style of the good God is not to produce a spectacle: God acts in humility.
—Pope Francis, homily, March 9, 2015

Nowadays, most candidates for U.S. president are multimillionaires, and the median net worth of members of the U.S. Congress is over one million dollars. Because the median net worth for the average American household is just over $50,000 (U.S. Census Bureau, September 2014), it is no wonder that candidates always seem to go out of their way to describe their humble beginnings. While this has been going on since the wealthy William Henry Harrison successfully portrayed himself as the "log cabin candidate" and was elected as our ninth president, today more than ever, voters—who tend to want to vote for people who are like themselves—are sensing a widening economic gap between themselves and their elected leaders. In an effort to bridge that gap, multimillionaire candidates from both political parties often stress their "blue-collar values" and tell stories of their parents' struggles to make ends meet, to earn a paycheck, and to put food on the table. They appear on the campaign trail in flannel shirts, rolled-up sleeves, blue jeans, and work boots and speak in an "aw shucks" manner to try to convince voters that they're "jus' folks."

Voters aren't the only ones sensing a widening gap between themselves and their leaders. Today in the church, the lay faithful sense a widening gap between themselves and church hierarchy. But that began to change the day that Cardinal Jorge Bergoglio was elected Pope. First, when it was announced that he had chosen the name Francis, it became immediately clear that the new pontiff was embracing simplicity and humility. In the following hours and days, this was reinforced by the many images of Pope Francis that we encountered through the media.

- He appeared on the balcony for the first time as pope wearing only the white cassock and simple black shoes, eschewing the red cape with furry trim and the red shoes of his predecessor.
- He boarded the minibus with the other cardinals to head back to the hotel instead of being chauffeured in a papal limo.
- He went to the hotel desk to pay for his own hotel bill.
- He chose to move not into the papal palace but into the much simpler papal apartments.
- He continued to skip the papal limo in favor of the much less ostentatious Ford Focus.
- Images from his previous life in Buenos Aires showed him riding public transportation on a regular basis.

It became clear that Pope Francis was communicating a new image for the church—a simpler, more humble church that was closer to the poor of the world. Before long, he made news by "firing" a German bishop known as "Bishop Bling," who had reportedly spent over $40 million on his own residence. He did the same with a Brazilian bishop who had spent over $600,000 on renovations to his residence and offices. Pope Francis recognized that if we are going to be a church on the move, we need to project an image of living simply—from the top down.

Cardinals, bishops, and clergy in general were put on notice: the church must avoid any perception of extravagance and instead must embrace simplicity to better identify with those who are poor. Pope Francis criticized what he called "airport bishops," who seem to prefer jet-setting to shepherding their flocks. He warned bishops and cardinals to avoid a "psychology of princes." When the Vatican ambassador, Archbishop Carlo Maria Viganò, spoke to U.S. bishops at their national meeting in 2013, he warned them that their efforts would be undermined if they failed to live simply and said, "The Holy Father wants bishops in tune with their people" (November 11, 2013). Many have responded, such as Archbishop Blase Cupich of Chicago, who, upon his appointment to the Archdiocese, chose not to move into the Cardinal's Mansion along Chicago's elite "Gold Coast" but instead moved into the more modest Cathedral rectory.

Many bishops and priests are following this example and are opting for less elegant living arrangements, driving more-modest cars, wearing less extravagant vestments, and eschewing French cuffs and cufflinks that gave them the appearance of corporate CEOs or royalty. I applaud these efforts and encourage pastors and bishops to continue making statements such as these. However, throughout this book I have attempted to demonstrate what parishes can do, not just what pastors can do! So with that in mind, I propose that parishes begin campaigns to encourage all parishioners to live more simply. A good way to inaugurate such efforts is to arrange for parishioners to read Susan Vogt's excellent book, *Blessed by Less: Clearing Your Life of Clutter by Living Lightly.* The parish can commit to reading and discussing the book over a period during which everyone—pastor, staff, and parishioners—attempts to live more simply in the spirit of Pope Francis. Vogt's strategies for living more simply include but are not limited to the following:

- eliminating clutter and excess possessions
- consuming less
- limiting time spent on social media
- giving away possessions
- simplifying your wardrobe
- limiting buying habits
- eating out less often and brown-bagging it more
- buying secondhand
- spending more time in nature
- purchasing fair-trade products

Vogt emphasizes that living simply is a spiritual principle at the heart of Ignatian spirituality. St. Ignatius of Loyola insisted that one of the keys to spiritual wellness is detachment from the things and worries of this world that might distract us from pursuing our ultimate purpose in life, which is to deepen our relationship with God. A church on the move needs to unload a lot of the excess baggage that is weighing us down and slowing us down.

Our human and planetary lives need many things to survive, but the more we can free ourselves from undue attachments to things that will pass away, the deeper our happiness will be.
—Susan Vogt, *Blessed by Less*

Questions for Reflection and Discussion

- Who are some current examples of politicians running for office and emphasizing their humble beginnings?
- What examples of simplicity and humility from the life of Pope Francis most impress and inspire me?
- What can I be doing right now to simplify my life?
- Why is detachment from material goods such a key spiritual principle?

From Stationary Fortresses of Guarded Grace to Mobile Units of Graced Encounters

---

Each Christian and every community must discern the path that the Lord points out, but all of us are asked to obey his call to go forth from our own comfort zone in order to reach all the "peripheries" in need of the light of the Gospel.
—Pope Francis, *Evangelii Gaudium*, 20

In 2010, when the Chicago Blackhawks won the Stanley Cup for the first time in forty-nine years, Chicagoans were delighted to learn that as part of the celebration, every member of the Blackhawks organization was entitled to spend one full day with the Stanley Cup, taking it anywhere he desired and doing anything he wanted with it. It was striking to see what these superstar hockey players chose to do with the Cup: many placed their newborn children in it; some ate cereal or ice cream sundaes out of it; others drank champagne, wine, or beer out of it; still others took it fishing with them, and one player even had his horse eat out of it. For the most part, players sought to wed this extraordinary Cup to their ordinary, everyday lives. In addition to that, over the course of the summer, the Stanley Cup popped up all over Chicagoland with opportunities for ordinary folks to stand next to it, kiss it, embrace it, and have their picture taken with it. I, along with a few thousand of my best friends, had such a wonderful opportunity when the Cup came to Incarnation Catholic Parish in a nearby suburb through the generosity of parishioner Mike Gapski, the Blackhawks' trainer. Ordinary people finally got to encounter this extraordinary piece of hardware.

For too many Catholics, the grace of God is as elusive and remote as the Stanley Cup was for those Chicago Blackhawks fans for nearly fifty years. We tend to portray God's grace as something that is heavily guarded and permanently located in the fortresses we call our parish churches. Our approach to "doing church" has led most folks to feel that God's grace is remote and is not something they can encounter in the ordinariness of their lives. If we are going to become a church on the move, we need to move from being stationary fortresses of guarded grace to mobile units of graced encounters. Just as members of Stanley Cup-winning teams take the trophy out of its storage place in Toronto and bring it to places where ordinary people can encounter it, our Catholic parishes need to identify ways of "bringing" God's grace out of the fortresses of our church buildings and into places where ordinary people can encounter it and recognize that it was there all along. And the most ordinary place to begin finding God is within our homes.

In the early church there was no such thing as a church building. The church—the people of God—gathered in homes, devoting themselves to "the apostles' teaching and to fellowship, to the breaking of bread and to prayer" (Acts 2:42). God's presence was encountered in the most ordinary of places: people's homes. I propose that we find new ways to bring the sacred into people's homes. Parishes can

- contact families and invite them to host an adult faith gathering—for example, a viewing and discussion of an episode of

Bishop Robert Barron's *Catholicism* (Word on Fire) or a segment of *Meaningful Conversations about Prayer* (Loyola Press) or other such programs. This could be an especially effective evangelization strategy to make a connection with a new family in the parish or neighborhood because they are basically being asked to provide hospitality to neighbors. Most people would be honored to be asked and to host such a gathering, and many people who might not come to a parish hall for such a gathering would consider going to a neighbor's home.

- arrange to pray the Liturgy of the Hours in different people's homes on various days and at various times of the day.
- arrange for the Way of the Cross to be prayed in people's homes during Lent.
- organize small faith-sharing groups and Bible-study groups to meet in homes, as discussed in chapter 39.
- conduct listening sessions in people's homes, as discussed in chapter 47.
- combine some of the above with light refreshments, including wine and cheese, in order to extend hospitality to all who gather.

One of the critical lessons of the Jewish people's years of wandering in the desert was their realization that their God was mobile. Previously it had been thought that gods were local and stationary (which explains why Jonah thought he could escape God by getting on a boat). The Jewish people, upon being led from slavery in Egypt to freedom, were delighted to learn that this awesome God who freed them was mobile. They happily carried God's presence—symbolized in the Ark of the Covenant—with them wherever they went as they wandered the desert for forty years. It is no wonder that God objected when David sought to build a temple, saying, "I have not dwelt in a house from the day I brought the Israelites up out of

Egypt to this day. I have been moving from place to place with a tent as my dwelling" (2 Samuel 7:5–6).

In many ways, we have once again relegated God to a geographic space, denying his "mobility" and creating the notion that, to encounter and experience intimacy with God, one needs to spend more time on the parish campus. If we are truly going to become a church on the move, then we need to get moving—off campus and into people's lives to help them discover the God who is already there. No doubt, this is why the Mass ends with the word *Go!* We're supposed to be on the move!

———————————

Spending more time in church doesn't make you a Christian any more than spending more time in a garage makes you a car.
—Anonymous

———————————

Questions for Reflection and Discussion

- What experiences have led me to feel that God's grace is remote? What experiences have led me to recognize that God's grace is near to me?
- Would I consider hosting a faith experience in my home, such as a faith-formation gathering, Liturgy of the Hours, the Way of the Cross, or listening sessions? Why or why not?
- What other faith enrichment experiences might parishes offer in people's homes?
- Why did the Israelites feel a special intimacy with God in the desert, and why did God object to the notion of a temple being built for him?

A New Kind of Army and a Different Kind of War

St. Ignatius of Loyola always wanted to be someone "on the move." He grew into adulthood with a burning desire to march into battle as a brave and heroic soldier, which he did, until a cannonball shattered his knee in battle. This did not stop Ignatius from being "on the move," however. He simply switched armies and went into battle as a brave and heroic soldier for Christ, working to build a church on the move.

Many of us are not unlike the young Ignatius: eager for a good fight. In the United States, for example, we seem to appreciate going into battle as much as did a young Ignatius; as a country, we have been at war 222 years out of the 239 years of our existence (as of 2015). It is no coincidence that Catholics never sing louder than when we are invited to sing the "Battle Hymn of the Republic" or "America the Beautiful" or "God Bless America" at Mass on a patriotic holiday such as Independence Day or Veterans Day. We are eager to march (or at least send our troops marching) into battle for what we believe is a noble cause.

It is time for us to take a page out of St. Ignatius's book and recognize that we are fighting the wrong battles. Yes, we are called to be on the move and marching into battle, not with weapons of destruction that incinerate the world but armed instead with the armor of God and the weapons of love, mercy, compassion, hope, and forgiveness—these are the weapons that will set the world on fire with God's love.

Our church has been weakened and is in retreat. It is time for us to retool and begin recruiting a whole new generation of warriors eager to march under the banner of a noble cause: the establishment of God's kingdom. It's time for us to become a church on the move inspired by God's triumph over sin and death through the resurrection of his Son, Jesus Christ.

Through the intercession of St. Ignatius of Loyola, may God give us the grace to get moving!

August 6, 2015
Seventieth Anniversary of the Bombing of Hiroshima

52 Ways to Get Mission and Mercy in Motion—At a Glance

1. Focus on brokenness.
2. Create an atmosphere of urgency.
3. Sing at every parish gathering.
4. Create discipleship pledge cards.
5. Focus on increased presence in people's lives.
6. Make Jesus' death and resurrection the center of parish life.
7. Promote Catholic practices.
8. Cultivate spiritual wellness.
9. Foster a robust Catholic identity.
10. Rely on consensus building for major decisions.
11. Flaunt diversity.
12. Conduct worshipful work at parish meetings.
13. Empower adults to mentor one another in faith.
14. Articulate expectations of parishioners.
15. Make all parish venues more welcoming.
16. Foster healing from the sex-abuse crisis.
17. Develop a flourishing online presence.
18. Change your parish appreciation dinner to a "Celebration of Ministries."
19. Enlist young adults in leadership positions.
20. Foster dialogue over current events pertaining to the Catholic faith.
21. Engage all the senses in worship experiences.
22. "Warm up" the congregation before Mass.
23. Infuse worship with more silence.
24. Liven up the music.

25. Fashion more energetic and frequent processions.

26. Form a homily committee.

27. Institute an offertory ritual to replace collection baskets.

28. Promote drinking from the cup at communion.

29. Mobilize the "troops" after communion.

30. Foster worship at parish gatherings.

31. Implement faith formation that is powered by works of mercy rather than doctrine.

32. Make adult faith formation a bona fide priority.

33. Keep it simple.

34. Empower parents to be their children's primary educators.

35. Offer variety for adult faith formation.

36. Get adults talking to one another.

37. Train adults in leadership/facilitator skills.

38. Hire college students to serve as catechists.

39. Form small faith-sharing groups.

40. Teach adults to pray as adults.

41. Help adults learn how to listen for God's voice.

42. Connect adult faith formation to everyday living.

43. Shift parish focus to serving the needs of the poor above all else.

44. Promulgate a consistent ethic of life.

45. Go green.

46. Invite people to heroic living.

47. Connect with people where they are.

48. Teach people how to share their stories of faith.

49. Begin a door-to-door ministry.

50. Focus parish attention outward.

51. Encourage living simply.

52. Take the "show on the road"—into people's homes.

Bibliography

Benedict XVI. *Deus Caritas Est.* 2005. www.vatican.va.

Berger, Jonah. *Contagious: Why Things Catch On.* New York: Simon & Schuster, 2013.

Biro, Brian D. *Beyond Success: The 15 Secrets to Effective Leadership.* Hamilton, MT: Pygmalion Press, 1995.

Brennan, Patrick J. *The Evangelizing Parish: Theologies and Strategies for Renewal.* Allen, TX: Tabor Publishing, 1989.

Bridges, Jerry. *Respectable Sins: Confronting the Sins We Tolerate.* Colorado Springs: NavPress, 2007.

Catechism of the Catholic Church. 2nd ed. Washington, D.C.: Libreria Editrice Vaticana, April 16, 2000.

Code of Canon Law. Washington, D.C.: Canon Law Society of America, 1999.

Congregation for the Clergy. *General Directory for Catechesis.* Washington, D.C.: United States Conference of Catholic Bishops, January 15, 1997. www.vatican.va.

Evans, Rachel Held. "Want Millennials Back in the Pews? Stop Trying to Make Church 'Cool.'" *Washington Post.* April 30, 2015.

Francis. *Evangelii Gaudium*. Washington, D.C.: USCC Bishops, December 13, 2013. www.vatican.va.

———*Laudato Si*. 2015. www.vatican.va.

General Instruction of the Roman Missal. Washington, D.C.: ICEL, 2012.

Gladen, Steve. *Small Groups with Purpose: How to Create Healthy Communities*. Grand Rapids, MI: Baker Books, 2011.

Goodstein, Laurie. "U.S. Bishops Struggle to Follow Lead of Francis." *New York Times*, November 11, 2014.

Halbach, Dr. Matthew. "What Parables Can Teach the Synod Fathers and the Church Today." Washington, D.C.: *Catechetical Leader*, March 2015.

Hyde, Douglas. *Dedication and Leadership*. South Bend, IN: University of Notre Dame Press, 1966.

John Paul II. *Evangelium Vitae*. Boston: Pauline Books & Media, May 1, 1995. www.vatican.va.

Keating, Thomas. *Invitation to Love: The Way of Christian Contemplation*. London: Bloomsbury Academic, 1994.

Kotter, John P. *Leading Change*. Boston: Harvard Business School Press, 1996.

Longbottom, Henry, SJ. "An Overview of Laudato Si." *Jesuit Post*, June 18, 2015.

Lowney, Chris. *Heroic Leadership: Best Practices from a 450-Year-Old Company That Changed the World*. Chicago: Loyola Press, 2005.

———*Heroic Living: Discover Your Purpose and Change the World*. Chicago: Loyola Press, 2009.

Lumen Gentium (Dogmatic Constitution on the Church). 1964. (www.vatican.va)

Mallon, Fr. James. *Divine Renovation: Bringing Your Parish from Maintenance to Mission*. New London, CT: Twenty-Third Publications, 2014.

Musicam Sacram (Instruction on Music in the Liturgy). 1967. (www.vatican.va)

National Directory for Catechesis. Washington, D.C.: USCCB, 2005.

Olson, Lindsay. "7 Simple and Smart Reasons to Hire Millennials." *U.S. News & World Report*, June 20, 2013. http://money.usnews.com/money/blogs/outside-voices-careers/2013/06/20/7-simple-and-smart-reasons-to-hire-millennials.

Our Hearts Were Burning within Us: A Pastoral Plan for Adult Faith Formation in the United States. Washington, D.C.: USCCB, 1999.

Packard, Josh, Ph.D. and Ashley Hope. *Church Refugees: Sociologists Reveal Why People Are Done with Church but Not Their Faith*. Loveland, CO: Group Publishing, 2015.

Paprocki, Joe, DMin. *A Well-Built Faith: A Catholic's Guide to Knowing and Sharing What We Believe*. Chicago, IL: Loyola Press, 2008.

———*Practice Makes Catholic: Moving from a Learned Faith to a Lived Faith*. Chicago, IL: Loyola Press, 2011.

Paul VI. *Evangelii Nuntiandi*. Boston: Pauline Books & Media, December 8, 1975. www.vatican.va.

Pew Research Center. "America's Changing Religious Landscape." May 12, 2015. www.pewforum.org/2015/05/12/americas-changing-religious-landscape.

Rainer, Thom S. *Autopsy of a Deceased Church: 12 Ways to Keep Yours Alive*. Nashville: B&H Publishing Group, 2014.

Ratzinger, Joseph Cardinal. *The Spirit of the Liturgy*. San Francisco: Ignatius Press, 2000.

Regan, Jane. "Toward Effective Adult Faith Formation." Adapted from *Gathering Together*. Chicago: Loyola Press, 2004.

Rohr, Richard. *Silent Compassion: Finding God in Contemplation*. Cincinnati: Franciscan Media, 2014.

Sanford, John. *Dreams: God's Forgotten Language*. Philadelphia: Lippincott, 1968.

Seeger, Eric. "The 7 Habits of Highly Effective Partners," *The Legal Intelligencer*, Mar. 23, 2009.

Silk, Mark. "White Christians Are Pro-torture, Nones Are Anti-. How Come?" *Religion News Service*, December 17, 2014.

Smith, Gary, SJ. *Radical Compassion: Finding Christ in the Heart of the Poor*. Chicago: Loyola Press, 2002.

Spadaro, Antonio, SJ. "A Big Heart Open to God: The Exclusive Interview with Pope Francis." *America*, September 30, 2013.

Sparough, Michael, SJ, Manney, Jim, and Hipskind, Tim, SJ. *What's Your Decision? How to Make Choices with Confidence and Clarity: An Ignatian Approach to Decision Making*. Chicago, IL: Loyola Press, 2010.

Stewardship: A Disciple's Response—A Pastoral Letter on Stewardship. Washington, D.C.: USCCB, 2003. www.usccb.org/upload/stewardship-disciples-response-10th-anniversary.pdf.

Taylor, Barbara Brown. *The Preaching Life*. Cambridge, MA: Cowley Publications, 1993.

Vogt, Susan V. *Blessed by Less: Clearing Your Life of Clutter by Living Lightly*. Chicago: Loyola Press, 2013.

Weber, Jeremy. "New Research Reveals Why People Visit Church Websites." *Christianity Today*, May 31, 2012.

Weber, Kerry. "Why 'Laudato Si' Is the Perfect Encyclical for Millennials," *America*, June 18, 2015.

White, Michael and Corcoran, Tom. *Rebuilt: Awakening the Faithful, Reaching the Lost, and Making Church Matter.* South Bend, IN: Ave Maria Press, 2012.

Winseman, Albert L. *Growing an Engaged Church: How to Stop "Doing Church" and Start Being the Church Again.* New York: Gallup Press, 2007.

Acknowledgments

I would like to thank the following people: Joe Durepos for always urging me on to write the next book; Ray Ives for providing me with insights on mobilizing parishes in social media; Fr. David Loftus, Fr. Jerry Gunderson, and Fr. Bill Hanson for reading my manuscript and offering valuable feedback from a pastor's point of view; Deb Breakey and the people of St. Cajetan Parish in Chicago for allowing me to propose and test ideas for reaching out to parents in their religious education program; Fr. Larry Sullivan and the staff and people of Christ the King Parish in Chicago for inviting me to propose and test ideas for adult faith formation; Vinita Hampton Wright for stellar editing; my brother John (Horse) Paprocki for creating the nifty little "Church on the Move" logo used in this book; and my wife, Jo, for "midwifing" another book to birth.

About the Author

Joe Paprocki, DMin, is National Consultant for Faith Formation at Loyola Press. He has thirty-five years of experience in ministry and has taught at many different levels. Paprocki is a popular speaker and the author of numerous books, including *Living the Mass, A Well-Built Faith,* and *7 Keys to Spiritual Wellness.* Joe serves as a catechist in the Archdiocese of Chicago and blogs about the experience at www.catechistsjourney.com.